SURFING GUIDE

TO

SOUTHERN CALIFORNIA

by

Bill Cleary and David H. Stern

Published by

Cleary and Stern
P. O. Box 5124
Santa Barbara, CA 93150

Distributed by

Block Surf   and   Mountain & Sea
P. O. Box 3483   P. O. Box 126
Chatsworth, CA 91313   Redondo Beach, CA 90277

CREDITS

Aerial Photos .... Eduardo and Lola Ricci
Maps .... Colin Cantwell
Cover Photo of Bill Cleary .... Jacobus "Co" Rentmeester
Cover Design .... Wes Herschensohn
Surfing Photos .... Credited in text

ACKNOWLEDGEMENTS
(1963)

The authors and publishers wish to thank the following surfers for their assistance, advice and constructive criticism during the gathering and editing of the information contained in this book: Carl Adamson, Hobie Alter, Ron Althouse, Wes Armand, O. W. "Blackie" August, Joe Barca, Brad Barrett, Eugene Brady, James Budge, Bob Burns, Robin Calhoun, Bill Collins, Bob Cooper, Will Cooper, Mike Cundith, Mike Dobransky, Alden and Ken Doesburg, Phil Edwards, Doug Erickson, Adrian Esnard, Robert Feigel, Jim Fitzpatrick, Mike Gaughan, Don Gilliam, Gary Glenn, Gary Goodwin, Robin Gustafson, John and Phil Hawley, Bob Hogan, Dempsey Holder, Arlen Knight, Darryl Kniss, Merv Larson, Harry "Butch" Linden, Willie Lippincott, Anthony Lloyd, Stan Matesich, Ken McWilliams, Rusty Miller, Mickey Muñoz, Harris Nelson, Greg Noll, Dave Olson, Mike O'Neil, Lee Peterson, Roy Porello, Jim "Mouse" Robb, Richard Roche Jr., Georges Samama, Darryl Stolper, Phil Stubbs, Don Thomas, Wayne Tompkins, Robert "Smitty" von Sternberg, Mike Waco, Leslie Williams, Reynolds Yater and many others.

Of these we express special gratitude to Bob Cooper and Phil Stubbs for both the quantity and quality of their surfing information. We are also grateful to officials of the California State Division of Beaches and Parks, and to the lifeguard services of San Diego and Los Angeles Counties and those of the cities of Santa Monica, Los Angeles, Huntington Beach, Long Beach, Newport Beach, San Clemente and San Diego. The California State Chamber of Commerce as well as those of several cities were helpful, and the United States Surfing Association provided much encouragement along the way. Without the help of people interested in the best possible future for surfing this book could not have been written.

DEDICATION TO THE
MEMORY OF JAMES FITZPATRICK

Topanga was the first and last place I ever lived that was truly home. The beach was my family. Over the years, though its members changed, the family was constant, as ever a family must be: it was there then even as it is there today, although the houses have been gone for more years than I care to number.

At day's end everyone gathered for the sunset, and after we had caught up on the day's events, the talk invariably turned to the surf. Was there a swell? How big? Who got the wave of the day? It didn't matter if you surfed or not — surfing was the dark adventure that bound us together. The waves rose over the outer reefs, endlessly tracing and retracing the invisible bottom like the hand of some ancient physician seeking the boundaries of the human soul.

One evening as the sun went down, Fitz turned to me and said, "I've got an idea. I think you are going to like it." And that was it, that was the moment this book began. And one by one, we all took our places in its story.

Fitz worked in the Hollywood dream factory; he was older than we were, but not really — people like Fitz stay young forever because they live in their dreams. He was the book's first publisher, but he was at heart a romantic, a storyteller, a man for whom everything was possible. He was an American visionary who thought everyone should throw out their trash on the freeway, so that the unemployed could get jobs picking it up. He imagined supermarkets on wheels that brought shopping for groceries to your neighborhood street corner. He had a quick and sensitive eye, a taste for beautiful women, a love for adventure. His quick Irish smile belied the hungry genius of a sidewalk sketch artist for that telling line of the jaw, a gesture, or a single line of dialogue that in one quick stroke would mark his subject's character as unique. (See Fitz's biographical sketch of the authors on page 8.)

Fitz invented his own niche in the Hollywood ghetto. His life was a movie within the movie, whose characters were the all too familiar examples of man's ignobility. There were tales of the California gold mines and gamblers and swindlers, stories that sprang out of the dark side of man's nature — but no matter how bleak they were, Fitz turned them to comedy and always left you feeling the essential goodness of humanity.

If he believed in something or someone, you never stopped hearing about it. Fitz had a million ideas, and they were already alive in him. He had the gift — this book is proof of it. Sure, I did my part; and David did his; but the magic in it was, and still is, Fitz's.

A few years later I was making money, I drove a Porsche and put locks on the gate. Fitz came by to talk but couldn't get in. He was appalled. "Cleary!" he yelled. "You're possessed by your possessions!"

Fitz was a free man and made no claim to owning anything. If you needed something he had, it was yours — and he gave everyone his heart.

3

Fitz's most poignant story was his own. In World War II he strayed behind Japanese lines and was surprised in the act of relieving himself by a Japanese soldier. Fitz disarmed him and almost got him to surrender, but at the last minute he had second thoughts and attacked Fitz, who mercifully dispatched him. Fitz would tell that story, and people would laugh till they cried — but the nightmares never left Fitz, who anguished over the fate of his slain adversary's family the rest of his life.

Only six years after the *Surfing Guide to Southern California* was published, in January of 1969, Fitz died of a heart attack at the age of thirty-nine. He left behind a whole beach full of people who will never forget him. David and I dedicate this 35th-Anniversary Nostalgia Edition to him.

Santa Barbara, August 1998   Bill Cleary

PREFACE TO THE ORIGINAL EDITION

The sport of surfing is booming all over the world and is destined to grow increasingly popular each year, the only limit being the total number of rugged individualists who will seek the satisfaction of doing something well and doing it better next time. It is a competitive sport, but the contest is between the individual and his own capabilities, and the victories are purely personal triumphs. It is not a team game, and there are no rules, regulations, scoring methods, or stadiums filled with cheering thousands. But whenever and wherever one of the uninitiated first stands upon his board and feels it slide forward down the face of a wave, the sport has gained another follower who is hooked for life. And when you multiply that feeling by all the undiscovered waves on all the ocean shores of the earth, you can realize the sport's potential.

Like boating and mountain climbing, it has attracted enough followers to support the publication of several good magazines. Like skiing, it offers sufficient visual excitement to be the subject of successful motion pictures produced for an audience of aficionados. Already it has its heroes, old-timers and legends, its own language and code of ethics, and its special kind of problems. One of its major growing-pains is overcrowding at a few well-known spots, which leads to other problems, such as misconduct on the part of a minority, which leads to official pressure on all surfers. Though our book describes these popular spots in full detail, we also hope it will help break the mob habit. On a hot Sunday in July there may be 100 surfers at Windansea, 300 at Malibu and 500 at Doheny; yet within a few miles of these congested beaches are uncluttered waves wasting their concave faces on deserted shores. This is ridiculous, but we are not about to mount a soapbox to champion the cause of spreading out. We feel the advantages should be evident to the individual, so we have limited ourselves to gathering enough information on all spots — including those deserted shores — to help widen the surfer's horizon.

We have written this book for surfers who want to go surfing in Southern California. Whether you are an accomplished artist who regularly extends his toes over empty space with the greatest of ease, or an admitted novice who carts his vintage plank to the beach each weekend for another session of grim effort and inglorious wipeouts, you are always looking for a better wave. The main purpose of this book is to give you the information you need to find it.

We have grouped the three hundred or so surfing spots between Point Conception and the Mexican border into fourteen areas, each one a comfortable one to explore on a one-day trip. The section devoted to each area begins with an introduction to the general conditions found there, along with a map showing the spots and the access roads. Next we describe the spots, giving details about the size range of waves, direction of ride, type of break, wave shape, swell direction, hazards and miscellaneous items you might like to know when surfing at an unfamiliar place. For the more adventurous surfer we have included appendixes on the relatively virgin surfing areas in Baja California and the Channel Islands; Northern California is mentioned briefly on page 23.

The descriptions are illustrated by aerial photographs showing the coastline's shape and in some instances the surf. We shot nearly all of them from the angle that best shows the features on shore — from over the ocean looking downcoast toward the land. Leafing through the book, you can ima-gine yourself flying south from Point Conception to Tijuana Sloughs, checking out the spots ahead with occasional glances backward. More careful examination of these pictures will prove them easily worth a thousand words.

The surfing photos we have included show characteristic waves in use. However, as we all know, the surf at any spot can vary from day to day, so when you sample a new beach, you may find waves quite different from those we have pictured or described. The worst beaches have their good days, and the best ones have their bad days — that's surfing.

As time passes, new spots will be given names, conditions may change, new laws will be enacted, and the shape of California's coastline will be altered by new jetties, harbors and breakwaters. Also it is inevitable that among the thousands of separate facts collected, we may have included some errors — that's writing. If you know of any new developments that can aid in preparing up-to-date versions of this guidebook in the future, please send them to the publisher. As we pointed out in the acknowledgements, this book would not have been possible without the help of many dedicated surfers. As Volume One in the International Surfing Guidebook Series, which will describe and illustrate the world's surf, we hope this book will help both the artist and the novice to discover for himself the unlimited excitement and variety of surfing in Southern California.

Topanga Beach
May 1963

Bill Cleary
David H. Stern

5

PREFACE TO THE
35ᵀᴴ ANNIVERSARY NOSTALGIA EDITION

Thirty-six years ago, when there were still houses lining the Topanga Beach cove, as in the photo on the back cover, Bill Cleary lived in the cellar of Jim Fitzpatrick's house overlooking the surf. At 24, Bill was the "kahuna" of Topanga Beach, and Jim was a filmmaker and father of three: two girls and a thirteen-year-old surf-stoked grommet whose hero and surfing guru was Bill. I was living in a house a few doors up the beach, a 27-year-old chubby, bald economics professor who had taken up the sport less than two years before but was already collecting material in anticipation of writing "the big book on surfing."

Jim convinced Bill to write a guidebook to 101 Southern California surf spots (the Pacific Coast Highway was also known as Highway 101). Bill got to work, wrote a draft, asked me to edit and finance it, and immediately took off for Biarritz, France, where he was the first competent surfer ever seen, and the Canary Islands, where he was possibly the first surfer ever.

Once I got hold of Bill's manuscript, I not only began editing it but re-researched it, rewrote it, added surf photos, aerial photos and maps; and when I looked over what I had done and realized that I had also added some two hundred surf spots, there was no turning back. I had quite unconsciously assumed paternity of the book, justifying my actions on the ground that he who controls the purse controls the project. Given this self-deceptive logic, it seemed appropriate for me to list my name first on the cover and title page. This wrong against Bill is at last rectified by placing his name first in the present edition, which is a jointly-financed labor of love. The book has endured, and Bill and I are still good friends.

First published in 1963, the *Surfing Guide to Southern California* finally sold out its first printing of 5,000 copies by 1969. (It took that long because surfers don't read, they surf — at least, that's how it was then.) In 1977 Bank Wright, of "Mountain and Sea," Hermosa Beach, reprinted it and kept it in print until the mid-'80's; he has also overseen the production of this edition.

Since the original publication, we have lost a few surf spots: some were destroyed by coastal construction (Dana Point, for example, became a marina) and others by "deconstruction" (the waves destroyed POP Pier). Access roads changed. Public property became private, and private property became public. In consequence, some of the information in the book is no longer correct, since this is a reprint of the first edition, minus the 1963–64 tide tables and some other outdated matter. In addition, surfing itself changed radically — this book came from the era when the only "shortboard" was Jim Foley's seven-foot chopped-off longboard in Santa Cruz. "Aerials" and "floaters" were unknown, and the ultimate achievement in small-wave riding was hanging ten — but we leave all that to the surf mags. The one constant in the surfing equations is the waves.

After the *Surfing Guide to Southern California* was published in 1963, Bill became the editor of *Surf Guide Magazine*, the first major competition with *Surfer Magazine*, back in the mid-60's. After *Surf Guide*'s untimely demise, he became an editor at *Surfer*, went on to write for *Life Magazine*, then wrote another surf book, *The Young Wave Hunters*. He ghost-wrote the best-seller *Inside the FBI*, the first book to tell what really went on there under J. Edgar Hoover. He was a dairy-farmer in Costa Rica, a macadamia-nut farmer in Hawaii and Australia, and a health foods entrepreneur in New Zealand. Somehow he found time to father three children. He retired from business and now lives at the beach in Southern California with his wife Barbara and daughter Mariella. He is rushing to complete the last in a series of surf novels.

I stopped teaching economics at UCLA in 1963 and went through a period of searching for the Truth (in those days it was called "dropping out"). The search was consummated when, in 1972, I came to know Yeshua (Jesus) as Israel's Messiah. Since then I have written five books on Messianic Judaism (Judaism that includes Jesus) — the *Complete Jewish Bible*, the *Jewish New Testament, Jewish New Testament Commentary, Messianic Jewish Manifesto*, and *Restoring the Jewishness of the Gospel: A Message for Christians*. In 1979 I immigrated to Israel; I live in Jerusalem with my wife Martha and children Miriam and Daniel in a restored old-stone house with meter-thick walls, parts of which date from the Crusader period, 900 years ago. Waves are available 40 miles away at the Tel Aviv and Herzliya beaches; and by my own minimalist definition (a surfer must catch at least one wave per calendar year — otherwise he's an ex-surfer), I am at 62 still a surfer, but sometimes only barely — in 1996 it wasn't until midway through December that I caught exactly two waves, both wipeouts, and on the second one my leash broke. But then, as I swam in lazily through the Mediterranean's 72-degree winter water, I remembered that back when the *Surfing Guide to Southern California* came out, leashes didn't even exist. As for the "big book on surfing," it never got written; but I'm considering publishing my notes for it as a period piece.

Jerusalem, August 1998   David H. Stern

THE AUTHORS

If a publisher were deliberately to set out to select two men to work together as co-authors of a book he would have difficulty finding a more unlikely combination than David Harold Stern and William Sheridan Cleary.

They are complete opposites in everything that counts, being no more adaptable to double-harness than a lion and an elephant. The only things they have in common are Los Angeles as a birthplace, UCLA as an alma mater, and the fact that they both surf. Even then, Stern is a goofy-foot.

Stern graduated from UCLA in 1955, went on to Princeton for graduate work in economics, earning his M. A. in 1957 and his Ph. D. in 1960 at the tender age of 24, and returned to teach at UCLA: Lecturer in Economics, 1960–61; Assistant Professor of Business Administration, 1961 to date. Cleary graduated from UCLA in 1962 at the ripe old age of 23 and has no intention of following Stern's measured ascent up the academic ladder. He is still trying to decide what he wants to be when he grows up.

Stern must watch his diet. Cleary's mother thinks he is too thin. Cleary enlisted for two years in the U. S. Marines. Stern hasn't been drafted yet. Cleary responds to the emotional power of Beethoven. Stern digs the orderly logic of Haydn. Stern made the fifth ascent of the east face of Canada's Mount Robson. Cleary regards mountains only as a place to shoot deer. Stern can't stand guns. Outside of surfing they don't have enough similar interests or experiences to support the most simple kind of bull-session. Yet somehow they have remained friends through it all.

Stern is precise and thorough in his research and writing. Cleary is quick and tricky, with a tendency to fill the pages in the heat of inspiration and worry about the commas and colons later. Clearly they are not a team. They do not work well together. But for over a year they gathered facts and figures for this book, traveling up and down the coast (in separate cars in opposite directions) to surf the spots and pump the locals. They wrote and rewrote, arguing over every statement requiring an opinion — just like any two surfers anywhere — and at one point Cleary took off for Europe and introduced surfing to the astonished natives of the Canary Islands. Which is as unteamlike as you can get.

But this team wasn't selected. It just happened. Everyone connected with the publication of this book lives on the beach. And if you live on the beach in Southern California you become interested in surfing. Stern — in his quiet scholarly fashion — had been amassing surfing lore from all over the world since he first surfed in 1960, intending someday to write the Big Book, a project that still takes up all his non-surfing leisure time today. Cleary had been stoked since he was in high school, and he majored in English Literature with a vague plan of doing something in the Hemingway line. And it just happened that they lived on the same beach…and one evening they joined some neighbors gathered on the sand to watch the sun go down…and somebody suggested that someone should write a sort of guidebook or something about all the great surfing spots along the Southern California coast….

Topanga Beach, 1963   James Fitzpatrick

CONTENTS

Credits and Acknowledgements 2
Dedication to the Memory of James Fitzpatrick 3
Preface to Original Edition (1963) 4
Preface to 35th Anniversary Nostalgia Edition of 1998 6
The Authors (by James Fitzpatrick, 1963) 8

INTRODUCTION TO SURFING IN SOUTHERN CALIFORNIA

Distances Along the Coast Route 11
What is a Surfing Spot? 12
Public and Private Beaches 13
Swell Classification 14
Weather and Winds.................................... 15
Water Temperatures 15
Sea Life... 16
Historical Sketch 17

SURFING SPOTS OF SOUTHERN CALIFORNIA

Point Conception Area 22
Goleta Area.. 34
Santa Barbara-Carpinteria Area 44
North Ventura County Area 56
South Ventura County Area 70
North Bay Area....................................... 84
South Bay 106
Palos Verdes Peninsula................................ 118
North Orange County Area............................. 132
South Orange County Area............................. 150
North San Diego County Area 172
La Jolla Area... 188
Sunset Cliffs Area.................................... 212
Coronado-Imperial Beach Area 226
Appendix: The Channel Islands 236
Appendix: Baja California 240

Surfing Equipment and Services 244
Index to Surfing Spots 250

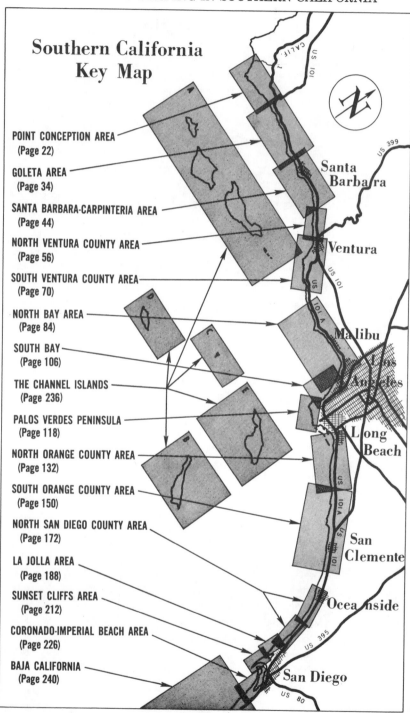

Southern California Key Map

POINT CONCEPTION AREA
(Page 22)

GOLETA AREA
(Page 34)

SANTA BARBARA-CARPINTERIA AREA
(Page 44)

NORTH VENTURA COUNTY AREA
(Page 56)

SOUTH VENTURA COUNTY AREA
(Page 70)

NORTH BAY AREA
(Page 84)

SOUTH BAY
(Page 106)

THE CHANNEL ISLANDS
(Page 236)

PALOS VERDES PENINSULA
(Page 118)

NORTH ORANGE COUNTY AREA
(Page 132)

SOUTH ORANGE COUNTY AREA
(Page 150)

NORTH SAN DIEGO COUNTY AREA
(Page 172)

LA JOLLA AREA
(Page 188)

SUNSET CLIFFS AREA
(Page 212)

CORONADO-IMPERIAL BEACH AREA
(Page 226)

BAJA CALIFORNIA
(Page 240)

Santa Barbara

Ventura

Malibu

Los Angeles

Long Beach

San Clemente

Oceanside

San Diego

CALIF 1

US 101

US 399

US 101

US 101 A

US 101

US 101 A

US 395

US 80

INTRODUCTION TO SURFING
IN SOUTHERN CALIFORNIA

The map on the opposite page shows the areas into which this guidebook divides Southern California. Following the distance table below is a comment on the use of the term "surfing spot" and a note on the problem of public and private beaches. Next comes a definition of "swell direction" with a description of the system surfers use to classify swells, and brief sections on wind and weather conditions, water temperatures and sea life. An illustrated five-page sketch of the history of Southern California surfing completes the introduction.

DISTANCES ALONG THE COAST ROUTE

The surfer's main drag is Highway 101, the Coast Route. The federal people call it U.S. 101-Alternate between Ventura and Capistrano Beach and insist the "true" 101 is an inland freeway, but except where confusion would result this guidebook uses the terms "Highway 101" and "Coast Route" interchangeably. In the following table the mileage figure opposite each place is the distance to the Mexican border along the Coast Route. To find the number of miles between any two towns in the table take the difference between the two numbers shown. Example: from Santa Monica to Huntington Beach is 149 − 108 = 41 miles.

(Point Conception*)	279	Wilmington (Palos	
Gaviota	259	Verdes south turn-off)	126
Tajiguas	252	Long Beach	121
Naples	244	Seal Beach	114
Goleta	239	Sunset Beach	111
Santa Barbara	231	Huntington Beach	108
Montecito	227	Newport Beach	102
Summerland	225	Corona del Mar	98
Carpinteria	220	Laguna Beach	91
La Conchita	214	Dana Point	85
Ventura	204	Capistrano Beach	83
Montalvo	200	San Clemente	78
Ventura Freeway turn-off		San Onofre	74
inland	198	Oceanside	55
Oxnard	195	Carlsbad	52
Port Hueneme turn-off	190	Leucadia	43
Solromar	176	Encinitas	42
Malibu	161	Cardiff-by-the-Sea	40
Topanga Beach	155	Solana Beach	38
Santa Monica	149	Del Mar	35
Venice	147	La Jolla north turn-off	29
El Segundo	140	Pacific Beach turn-off	24
Manhattan Beach	138	Sunset Cliffs turn-off	20
Hermosa Beach	136	San Diego (Coronado Ferry)	16
Redondo Beach	134	Chula Vista	9
Torrance Beach		Palm City	6
(Palos Verdes north turn-off)	132	San Ysidro	2
*Accessible only by private road		Mexican Border (Tijuana)	0

11

WHAT IS A SURFING SPOT?

The term "surfing spot" is misleading. It is physically possible to surf nearly anywhere along Southern California's coastline, the only exceptions being a few miles protected by breakwaters, a few miles where the rocky shore and bottom would deter anyone but an insane man, and a few miles (just how many depends on how desperate you are for a comber) which virtually never see waves big enough or good enough to ride. What, then, defines a surfing spot?

In the old days (i.e., fifteen or thirty years ago) the term meant just what it said—a spot, a small area where the waves were clearly more suited to boardriding than at locations only a short distance away. All the *point breaks* such as Malibu and Rincon and all the *reef breaks* such as Windansea and Paddleboard Cove fit this classical definition, as do a number of other "spots".

In those days the few surfers who tackled the ocean with their heavy unmaneuverable planks had little incentive to seek the short rides available on the waves usually found in front of long sandy beaches. But with the light boards of today this kind of surf is both fun and a challenge—it is no accident that many of the best small-wave riders have perfected their style reacting to the unpredictable waves of a *beach break*. Furthermore, with the surfer population increasing as if growth-curves were going out of style, the person who seeks uncrowded waves will often find he must search for them along a sandy beach.

At such a beach surfers may congregate at particular locations (for example, 22nd Street in Hermosa Beach), or access to some portions may be more convenient than to others (Hendry's Beach in Santa Barbara), or surfing may be legal at some areas and not at others (see examples in Newport Beach, Huntington Beach, San Diego and elsewhere). These become known as places to surf even though the waves there are no better (perhaps even worse) than those several hundred yards up or down the coast. But are they really surfing spots? Are surfing spots determined physically or socially? In this book we have played it by ear, using the names of surfing spots merely to assist in our primary goal, which is to describe conditions *everywhere* along the 80 or 90 percent of the coast where now and then are found ridable waves. It turns out that we distinguish about 285 spots between Point Conception and the Mexican border. Someone else using another method of classifying them might come up with an altogether different number.

While many spots are called by the names you can find on official maps, others have colorful names invented by surfers themselves. Some places are named for a characteristic of the surf: "Horseshoe" describes the shape of the wave as it bends around the reef into a bowl, "Avalanche" is what the white water does down the face of the wave on the south side of Lunada Bay, and taking off at the north point of Paddleboard Cove indeed feels like descending a "Ski Jump." Other names are derived from the persons who first surfed there (or rode there early and often)—"Renny's" (Reynolds Yater), "Perko's" (Bob Perko), "D & W's" (Mike Doyle and Lennie Wittemore), "K & G Point" (Al Kostler and

Leroy Golding), and, contrary to what you might think, "Bee Aye Point" (Dick Bendicksen and Al Kostler). Many places are named prosaically for a nearby street, prominent building or obvious natural feature, but even a few of these are interesting: "Crumple Car" described an auto wreck on the beach which has since washed away, "Burn-Down House" used to be called "Riviera Club" until . . . well . . . uh . . . it burned down. A few names are admissions of ignorance: "Secos" reflects an inability to spell, "Seven Jetties" an inability to count. Wherever possible we include all the names in common use as alternates, and all of them appear in the alphabetical index.

PUBLIC AND PRIVATE BEACHES

In California the ocean and the beach below the "mean high tide line"* belong to the state and are always available for use by surfers unless a local ordinance prohibits surfing at a particular time or place. However *access* to the public portion of the beach is quite another story. Owners of private beach-front property can forbid trespassing either personally or with fences and signs, and in some instances violation of their wishes is a misdemeanor as well as a civil offense. A surfer confronted by a property-owner asking him to leave has no choice but to do so. Owners sometimes allow surfers to trespass, but such an agreement has yet to result from an on-the-spot quarrel.

Where private property stretches unbroken along several miles of beach the public (that is, most surfers) are effectively prevented from reaching the ocean, except by paddling or walking below the mean high tide line from a public access point, the nearest of which may be miles away. The administrative and legal problems entailed in condemnation of strips of private land to provide access points at convenient intervals along the coast—as has been done in parts of Hawaii—lie beyond the scope of a guidebook. The point for surfers to note is that many of the surfing spots described in this book are not available for them to use. We have included them with the hope that some of them will eventually be opened up again, just as we hope none of the other spots we have described will be closed to the public.

Wherever possible we have indicated whether direct access to a surfing spot violates private property rights; however in some cases information about beach ownership was not available. The authors and publishers wish to make it clear that nothing contained in or implied by this guidebook is to be construed as encouragement to trespass; furthermore the authors and publisher disclaim all responsibility for the actions of any person who uses the information contained herein to further any illegal activity whatsoever.

*The determination of the "mean high tide line" at a particular place is a job best left to oceanographers and lawyers; for us to discuss it would be to open a legal Pandora's box.

SWELL CLASSIFICATION

One factor that causes one spot to have better surf than another on a particular day is the direction of the swell. By "swell" we mean the waves generated by the winds in a particular storm, for all waves that surfers ride are caused by winds at a distance blowing in the general direction of Southern California. A given swell may last a day, another a week. Two or more different swells may be present simultaneously.

Oceanographers have instruments to measure with great precision the characteristics of swells, but detecting them merely by observation from the beach is a fine art whose rules are not easily codified. Surfers realize, however, that the following classification system is very rough: "south" swells from slightly different directions can produce waves of very different size and quality at a given spot.

- **Summer Swell, South Swell, Southwest Swell.** Generated by storms in the South Pacific (most common between April and October) or by *chubascos* (hurricanes) off the coast of Baja California (June-November). Waves appear as strong clear lines. Size is commonly 2-5 feet but occasionally it exceeds 15 feet at a few places.

- **Winter Swell, West Swell, North Swell.** From storms in the North Pacific (October-April). Some of these storms lie south of due west, others farther north; at times surfers draw this distinction between "west" and "north" swells (the "west" swells are said to be more common during the fall months), while at other times the terms are used interchangeably. The lines are usually strong and clear, though not always. Typical size is 3-6 feet, and once or twice a year a couple of spots nudge 15-20. (Note: Point Conception itself keeps Southern California from receiving swells generated in and near the Gulf of Alaska. Of course a truly north swell is impossible; it would have to come barrelling down the Ridge Route from Bakersfield.)

- **Wind Swell, West Wind Swell.** Produced by prevailing winds within a few hundred miles of shore; these winds are often a little stronger after the passage of a cold front. This small uneven peaky surf (up to 4-5 feet) comes up the year round but is most noticed in spring.

- **Day-After-Storm Surf.** Generated by local storms. November-April is the usual season. Waves are typically close together and very uneven in appearance but can be quite large (up to 10 feet or more).

- **Wind Chop, Blown-Out Surf.** Waves produced by onshore winds blowing in the immediate vicinity of a surfing spot; characterized by bumpy appearance of the sea, whitecaps, and unhappy surfers. Wind chop can ruin the quality of otherwise excellent surf within minutes.

Unusual weather conditions somewhere in the Pacific can bring off-season swells, such as a south swell in January. There is no "best time of year" to surf apart from the most likely times for the storms that produce the waves.

WEATHER AND WINDS

The typical summer day at the typical Southern California beach starts off cloudy and windless, temperature near 60, surf glassy. Before noon the sky clears and the thermometer heads for the low 70's, but within an hour or two the sea-breeze commences, bringing unpleasant wind-chop to the majority of surfing spots. Sometimes it dies down an hour or two before sundown, allowing the surfer to enjoy an evening glass-off.

Winter days are five to ten degrees cooler but often clear and windless with glassy water all day. Also fall and winter are the seasons for occasional warm dry Santa Ana winds which blow offshore at most beaches, causing waves to be well-shaped and hard-breaking. Colder offshore winds may follow winter storms.

Though this brief description is true on the average, no guidebook can explain why one beach may be chilled by a foggy wind while another only a mile or two away is warm, clear and calm.

WATER TEMPERATURES

Water temperatures in Southern California are influenced by the California Current, a cold ocean-surface current flowing south from the Gulf of Alaska (not, as is popularly believed, by the warm Japanese Current, which, strange to say, is located not here but off the coast of Japan). The current, however, is quite far from the coast — beyond the Channel Islands — so that near the mainland the sun warms the water to temperatures considerably higher than that of the current itself. Roughly speaking, temperatures are in the 60's or low 70's in summer and in the 50's in winter. The following table gives representative figures.*

LOCATION	MONTHLY AVERAGES												COLDEST EVER RECORDED	WARMEST EVER RECORDED
	JAN	FEB	MAR	APR	MAY	JUN	JUL	AUG	SEP	OCT	NOV	DEC		
Santa Barbara	55	55	57	58	60	64	66	67	65	62	60	57	51	73
Port Hueneme	56	56	56	56	57	59	61	62	62	61	60	58	49	72
Santa Monica Pier	55	56	57	58	60	64	66	67	65	62	60	57	51	73
Los Angeles Harbor	56	57	58	59	61	63	66	67	65	64	61	58	50	76
Balboa Pier	57	57	58	59	61	64	66	67	65	64	61	59	50	77
La Jolla (Scripps Pier)	57	57	58	59	62	64	65	66	64	63	61	59	51	77

*Source: United States Coast and Geodetic Survey.

Here and there along the coast water wells up from colder ocean depths, examples, according to surfers, being found in the Point Conception area, at Arroyo Sequit, in Coronado, at Tijuana Sloughs, and, judging from the table above, at Port Hueneme in summer. Water temperatures are also likely to be low after a day or two of strong offshore winds.

SEA LIFE

Southern California waters contain little hazardous sea life. Dangerous sharks are very rare near the coast although harmless varieties are not uncommon. Killer whales, reputedly more vicious than any shark, are still rarer. However there are a number of annoying sea creatures to watch for.

Stingrays are found here and there along the coast especially in late summer. They lie on the bottom in the surf zone and can inflict a very painful wound in the foot of anyone unfortunate enough to step on one. The best way to avoid injury if stingrays are known to be present is to do as little walking in the water as possible—swim or paddle instead. If stung have the wound cleaned by a doctor because it infects easily. Treatment for shock is often necessary.

Jellyfish appear sometimes during the summer months. Their clear purple or blue umbrella-like floats are between 2 and 12 inches in diameter, but the tentacles which contain the stinging-cells may extend underneath for 15 or 20 feet—so give them a wide berth. If injured by one rub the affected part with clean wet sand, wash it with ammonia, and apply a good burn ointment.

Sea urchins are found wherever the tidal zone is rocky. They grow to be 2-6 inches in diameter and are covered with brittle purple spines. If you step on one the spines break off, and portions allowed to remain under the skin emit a poison which can make the wound hurt for months. It is therefore important to remove the spines very carefully. The easiest way, since they are composed of calcium carbonate, is to dissolve them in any weak acid such as vinegar, lemon juice or uric acid. The last suggests a possible emergency procedure.

Southern California has both good and bad seaweed. The "good kelp" grows in thick bands a quarter-mile to a mile offshore in water 15 to 50 feet deep. It cuts down wind-chop while allowing strong swells to pass, so that the protected surf stays glassy even while onshore winds blow. The "bad kelp" grows in water so shallow that it actually interferes with surfers trying to ride waves by catching skegs and inducing "surprise" wipeouts. Kelpcutters are able to harvest commercially the good kelp but not the bad kelp. Pity.

Seals are seen occasionally, porpoises and dolphins less often. Rarely dangerous unless bothered they enjoy surfing as much as humans and get some gassy rides!

The grunion is a small silvery fish which swims inshore by the millions a few days each month during spring and summer in order to lay eggs in the sand. Its significance for surfers is zero, except that after a wipeout swimming through a school of them tickles.

Actually, Southern California's ocean is rather friendly. The most hazardous form of sea life is found above the waterline paddling out in the wrong place, taking off from the wrong spot, crowding surfers out of waves, letting its board loose at the wrong time, and being a general menace wherever it goes. This species, the careless or thoughtless surfer, is the most dangerous of all—both to others and to himself.

HISTORICAL SKETCH

1900: Surfing is unknown in California and nearly dead in its homeland, Hawaii, after years of suppression. 1907: The revival of surfing at Waikiki is spurred by adventuring author Jack London, who that year writes an article for a national magazine in which he mentions "one Freeth." 1908: George Freeth is brought to Redondo Beach as a tourist attraction and there becomes the mainland's first known surfer. His first students: Louis E. Martin, Percy "Pink" Furlong, and Sidney Williams. 1912: Duke Kahanamoku, on his way from Hawaii to the Olympic Games, spots a likely curl, rides it, and so discovers Corona del Mar. Other places ridden in these infant years are Long Beach and Huntington Beach. 1919: Freeth dies of influenza, aged 35.

George Freeth surfing both forward and backward—Redondo Beach, 1914.
[Courtesy of Ray Kegeris]

George Freeth and 1910-type gremmies. Left to right: George Mitchell, Tommy Witt, Freeth, Ray Kegeris, Gerry Witt. [R. Lemon, courtesy of Lou Martin]

The 1920's: The Duke and his buddies are making movies in Hollywood but aren't too busy to join the gang at Corona del Mar now and then. Among the several dozen regulars are the Vultee brothers (who will one day be better known for their airplanes), Willie Grigsby, Haig Priest, Lee Jarvis, and newcomers Pete Peterson and Lorrin Harrison, who will still be winning tandem surfing contests in the 1960's. In 1926 Tom Blake invents the paddleboard in Santa Monica. 1927: Blake and Sam Reid cut virgin white trails across the waves at Malibu.

Above: The old Corona del Mar surf could be ridden left into Newport Bay or right, past the end of the jetty. Size of surf shown is about 8-10 feet, and waves here could reach 20 feet. Surf today still reaches this size on the far side of the west jetty —at the Wedge.
[Courtesy of Bob Reed]

Left: "What, me worry?" Mac Beall stands on the tail of his plank surfing alongside the old Corona del Mar jetty, while Gene "Tarzan" Smith, later to become the world's greatest distance paddler, watches lazily for another wave. The time, about 1933. [Courtesy of Bob Reed]

The 1930's: The Depression is on and jobs are scarce, so let's go surfing. Regular visits to Palos Verdes Cove, Long Beach "Flood Control," "Abalone" and "Garbage Chute" in Sunset Cliffs, "The Point" in Pacific Beach, "Killer" Dana. Tentative explorations at Rincon, Tijuana Sloughs, Swami's, Windansea. Pier-shooting at Huntington Beach, at Pacific Beach, at Venice (but that one's gone now). Tear-shedding over the destruction of the surf at Corona del Mar, and the clan moves to San Onofre. Eight or a dozen surf clubs competing in—what is it, anyway?—paddleboard-polo. 1932: The first crossing of the Catalina channel on paddleboards—by Tom Blake, Sam Reid and Wally Burton. Surfers like Lewis "Hoppy" Swarts, Bud Morrissey, Dorian Paskowitz, John Blankenship, Lloyd Baker, Bob "Hammerhead" Gravage, and Jim "Burrhead" Drever—all still known today but usually called "Mister" by those with whom they share the waves. Others like Gard Chapin, Adie Bayer, Tulie Clark, Al Bixler, and George "Nellie Bly" Brignell remembered by those who remember.

Paddleboard Cove around 1939, "when boards were made of wood and men were made of iron." E. J. Oshier and Leroy Grannis on planks and Adolph Bayer on his paddleboard at the "Ski Jump." [John H. "Doc" Ball]

San Onofre on a crowded Sunday in 1938. [Dr. Don James]

The 1940's: The surfers go to war and leave the waves to the kids. And who shall lead them? A skinny misanthrope with a crooked left arm, a nasal voice and an incisive mind, who refuses to believe that 120-pound planks are the ultimate achievement in surfboard technology. His name, Bob Simmons. His contribution, a light board with a skeg—easy to carry, easy to ride. To help him build them, Joe Quigg and Matt Kivlin. To ride the new boards, Dale Velzy, Bev Morgan, Bob Hogan and Leslie Williams —turning faster and tiptoeing gingerly toward the nose. 1954: According to a newspaper estimate there are 1500 surfers in Southern California. Three months later Simmons dies surfing at Windansea, and with him an era.

The good old days at Malibu — big waves, no crowds (in fact, as you can see, the public hardly knew what surfing was) . . . and the unmistakable form of Bob Simmons streaking in from the point. Date, about 1950. [Joe Quigg]

"The Sliding Contest" between Joe Quigg (left) and Bob Simmons, Malibu, 1950.

Then the explosion. 1956: The book "Gidget," about real surfers at real Malibu (except the movie was shot at Secos). 1956: Hobie Alter and Dave Sweet bring out "foamies," using polyurethane plastic instead of Simmons-era balsa. The surfing movies—first Bud Browne, then Bruce Brown and John Severson, then still others—fill the beach auditoriums with screaming mobs, and soon the inland auditoriums too. And a new generation of surfers perfect whip-turns and hanging ten, Quasimodos and head-dips, standing islands and reverse kickouts—Phil Edwards, Mickey Chapin (Dora), Dewey Weber, Mickey Muñoz, Rick Grigg, Tom Morey, Bobby Patterson, Alan Gomes, Buzzy Bent, Fred Pfahler, Mike Doyle, Kemp Aaberg, Lance Carson, Terry "Tubesteak" Tracy . . .

And suddenly surfing is a fad. In 1962, over 25,000 persons purchase new boards, and twice as many people buy copies of the "Surfer" magazine. A whole subculture arises among teen-agers based on dress, language, and invidious distinctions between surfers, ho-dads, gremlins and kooks (the Hawaiian antecedent of the last word having long been forgotten). Peroxide-blond kids carrying boards in their woody wagons identify with all the other peroxide-blond kids carrying boards in their woody wagons and feeling part of the "we" they raise hell they wouldn't even try to lift if each was only a "me." The incidents start in the surf and on the beaches and in the coast towns and cities, and while everyone blames the "other guys" the authorities react by closing one beach after another to surfing—to all surfers. As the sport grows the number of beaches available to surfers diminishes, and the individual is left to wonder, "Who's in charge here? What does it all mean?"

Even as some surfers—and some masquerading non-surfers—distort the public's image of the sport, other dedicated surfers support the United States Surfing Association, formed to preserve surfing from its abusers, to guide it through its willy-nilly adolescence, and to guide adolescents through surfing. In time the elements of surfing that make it a fad movement must die away, but the basic attraction of the sport— the lure of the waves—is eternal. From now on there will be an increasing number of persons who regard surfing as a healthful recreation as well as a smaller core of regulars to whom it is an all-consuming passion. The future of surfing depends on them—and you.

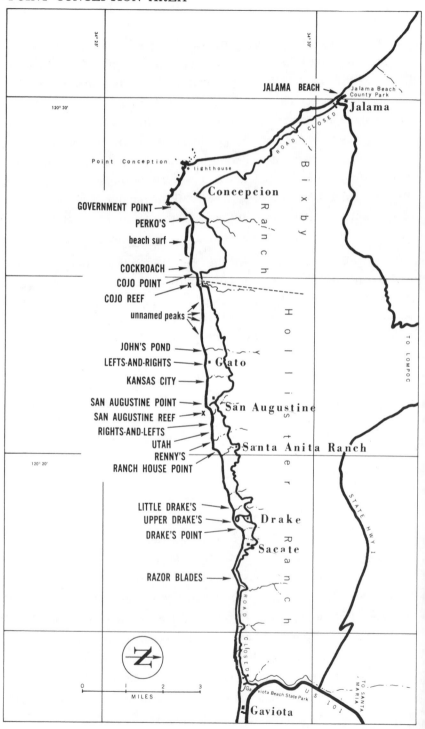

POINT CONCEPTION AREA

The 15 miles of coastline between Point Conception and Gaviota is owned by two families, the Bixbys and the Hollisters, and is closed to the general public. The Bixbys, whose property runs from Cojo northward past Point Conception to Jalama Beach, admit only personal friends. The Hollister Ranch (Cojo east to Gaviota) is open only to the 80 members of the Santa Barbara County Surf Club. They may not bring guests, and a 24-hour guard at the entrance gate is deputized to arrest trespassers. We have listed the surfing spots anyway, in the event the current situation should change.

Meanwhile the rest of us, rather than entering illegally or going away mad, might explore some of the excellent surfing areas north of Point Conception, although they lie outside the region covered in this guidebook. Such spots as **JALAMA BEACH** (off State Highway 1 between Las Cruces and Lompoc) and well-named **SURF BEACH** (west of Lompoc at the end of State Highway 150) are more consistently "up" than most places in Southern California. These are public, never crowded, and not more than an hour's drive from Gaviota.

Farther north are **POINT SAL, PISMO BEACH, AVILA, MORRO BAY, CAYUCOS POINT, CAMBRIA PINES, SAN SIMEON POINT, WILSON CREEK, BIG SUR RIVER MOUTH** and many more spots along 200 miles of relatively unexplored coastline culminating in the moody ocean-battered cliffs of Point Lobos. Beyond this wild area are the surfing beaches of **CARMEL, ASILOMAR, PACIFIC GROVE** and **MONTEREY,** followed by at least a hundred spots between **SANTA CRUZ** and **SAN FRANCISCO,** and still more places north of that. In fact there are so many great spots that the surf of Northern California will be the subject of another volume in the International Surfing Guidebook Series.

Returning south we find that Point Conception itself does break but is not really a surfing spot because of sheer cliffs and rocks which destroy boards and prevent easy access. The U.S. Government uses the immediate point area for a lighthouse and does not permit entry. The ridable beaches are described on the following pages.

Bixby Ranch. View from over the ocean, looking downcoast. (1) Government Point. Surf about 4 feet. Seven lines visible. (2) Perko's. (3) Beach surf. Barely breaking today. (4) Cockroach, Cojo Point and Cojo Reef. Coast in foreground is rocky and unsurfable. Point Conception is out of sight at left.

GOVERNMENT POINT—A right slide breaking over a sand and rock bottom. Wave has perfect shape but is not especially steep except for shorebreak. Takes any swell but north better. Surfable at any size and reaches 15 feet. Rides in winter are up to one-quarter mile in length, with a good lineup all the way.

PERKO'S—Right slide point break of medium length. Hollow peak take-off is followed by slow ride until zippy shorebreak. Ridable up to six feet. Takes south swell best.

UNNAMED BEACH BREAK—Small peaky swell produces fair beach surf. Waves over four feet tend to wall up and crash.

(1) Cockroach. (2) Cojo Point. Surf about 3 feet. (3) Cojo Reef. Swells can be seen peaking up inside and would break if bigger. Dark patches are kelp.

COCKROACH—Right slide into close-out at Cojo Point.

COJO POINT—Right slide over a slabby rock shelf. A very fast hollow tubular get-up-and-go wave. In smaller surf fast part of ride ends in middle of Cojo Bay but you can continue straight off for a long distance. At ten feet fast part of ride ends in whomping shorebreak. Takes a south swell and is considered one of the best summer spots on the Ranch; winter surf is smaller and poorer.

COJO REEF—Left or right from peak takeoff. Inside peak ridable from 3 to 10 feet. Small surf backs off after takeoff and ride is essentially straight in; larger surf is somewhat faster, but long rides are still rather mushy and tedious. Outer reef breaks at 10-plus feet and can become huge.

POINT CONCEPTION AREA

GOVERNMENT POINT.

Ken Kesson COJO POINT.

COJO REEF

ollister Ranch. (1) Kansas City. (2) San Augustine Point. (3) San Augustine Reef. (4) Rights-nd-Lefts. (5) Utah. Surf is running 3-4 feet. Lefts-and-Rights is just out of sight at left.

OHN'S POND (NOCHE'S)—The easternmost of several canyon mouths rhich have in front of them small unnamed ridable right-slide shore-reaks on a south swell. Inconsistent but good when up.

EFTS-AND-RIGHTS—Reef break offering rides implied by name. Best n south swell but also breaks on west. Closes out over 6 feet.

ANSAS CITY—Minor reef break with rights and lefts occasionally.

AN AUGUSTINE POINT—Not a point break, but a peak off the outer art of the point. Best in summer. Closes across to San Augustine Reef t 6 feet.

AN AUGUSTINE REEF—Hollow peak bowls up and backs off, so that creaming takeoff is followed by either giant cutback or shooting over op of wave in squat. Ridable to 15 feet, maybe more. Essentially a right lide, but lefts possible when small. High tide preferred because reef is hallow. West swell best. Location: 100 yards east of San Augustine 'oint.

IGHTS-AND-LEFTS—Lefts usually better. Breaks on west swell. Ridable ɔ 8 feet, then closes out.

POINT CONCEPTION AREA

Lefts and rights at LEFTS-AND-RIGHTS. [Gary Connelly]

Gary Connelly, LEFTS-AND-RIGHTS. [Bobby Hazard]

Gary Connelly peers into a LEFTS-AND-RIGHTS tube. [Bobby Hazard]

Alan Hazard drops from the peak at SAN AUGUSTINE REEF. [Gary Connelly]

Bob Cooper, the bearded bard, back-pedals from the nose at RIGHTS-AND-LEFTS.
[Richard Vincent]

Paddling out at RIGHTS-AND-LEFTS.

Extreme low tide reveals the eelgrass at RIGHTS-AND-LEFTS.

RIGHTS-AND-LEFTS. [Richard Vincent]

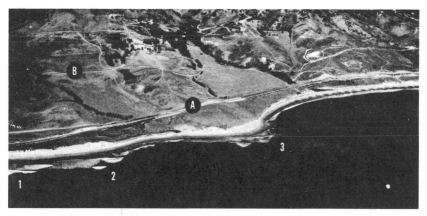

(1) Utah. (2) Renny's. (3) Ranch House Point. Kelp bands clearly visible. On land: (A) Railroad track. (B) Private road through the Hollister Ranch.

UTAH—Another canyon-mouth right slide best on a south swell and ridable to six feet.

RENNY'S—Also referred to by members as "You know that pipeline just above Ranch House?" Right slide ridable to 6 feet.

RANCH HOUSE POINT—Surf at large-scale point gets big on a south swell and looks good but consists of often unmakable sections followed by dull flat spots. Area in located below Hollisters' home, and club members may not drive onto this portion of beach.

RIGHTS-AND-LEFTS. [Richard Vincent]

POINT CONCEPTION AREA

Tom Caesar, LITTLE DRAKE'S. [Gary Connelly]

George Greenough kneels on his belly-board under the curl at UPPER DRAKE'S.
[Richard Vincent]

DRAKE'S POINT. [Richard Vincent]

LITTLE DRAKE'S (CRUMPLE CAR)—One of the most hollow "suckular" tubes on the Ranch; waves suck out over a rock shelf. Ridable to 8 feet, at which size place is hairy. Mainly a right; lefts possible when small. Offshore wind less common here than at other nearby spots. A winter break.

UPPER DRAKE'S—Right slide separated from Drake's Point proper by an unmakable section.

DRAKE'S POINT—A long right slide, best on west swell but also breaks on north; the main winter spot in the area. Ridable from 4 to 12 feet. A quality wave.

RAZOR BLADES (RAZORBACK, THIRD TRESTLE if you count the one at Gaviota, or **SECOND TRESTLE** if you don't)—Still another long right-slide point. Gets as big in winter as any place on the Ranch. Looks better than Drake's from cliff above, but rows of sharp slate sticking up inshore would annihilate boards and probably people.

A surfer paddles out, turns around and takes off on a long wall at UPPER DRAKE'S.
[Richard Vincent]

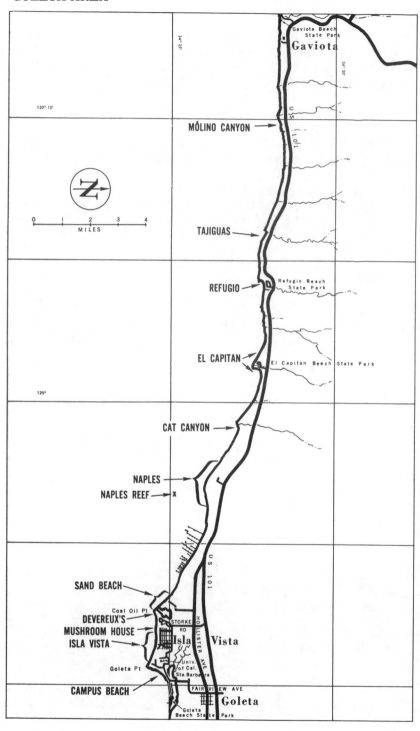

GOLETA AREA

Coastline runs east and west; thus south swells would hit directly were they not almost completely blocked off by the Santa Barbara Channel Islands. Thus the area receives mainly west swells, which move in along the coast at a 90-degree angle. Where the coast projects outward the swell hits the west side of the bulge and makes good beach surf, then wraps around the east side to make point surf. A substantial percentage of the total coastline rarely gets waves big enough to ride. Main town in area is Goleta, 8 miles west of Santa Barbara. Isla Vista lies just west. Tajiguas and Gaviota are tiny villages farther west. Campgrounds include Gaviota Beach State Park, 29 miles west of Santa Barbara, and Refugio (see below).

MOLINO CANYON—Right slide from peak just east of not very noticeable point takes a winter swell or a wind swell. Location: by Highway 101, 4 miles east of Gaviota Beach turn-off, and 6 miles west of Refugio Beach, near mouth of Molino Canyon.

TAJIGUAS—Peak break 2 miles west of Refugio Beach, near village of Tajiguas.

Garth Murphy fights a losing battle with the REFUGIO shorebreak. [Suzan Murphy]

Refugio. No visible surf, but swells show up well as they pass sharp jutting point. Amoeba-like white dots are surfers waiting for 3-foot sets. (A) U.S. Highway 101. (B) Slough at mouth of Refugio Creek.

REFUGIO BEACH STATE PARK (Locals pronounce it "Refufio")—Right slide point breaks both winter and summer but is inconsistent. Good peak takeoff is followed by well-shaped slow lineup which allows turning till you reach the fast hollow often walled-out shorebreak. Best at 3-4 feet; reaches 8 feet but is mushier then. Normal afternoon seabreeze blows offshore. Park is run by Santa Barbara County. Lifeguards on duty 10 AM to 6 PM daily in warmer months. Parking costs 50 cents, overnight camping one dollar. Dressing rooms, snack bar, grocery store. Location: on Highway 101, 19 miles west of Santa Barbara.

Richard Roche on the nose in the "fast hollow often walled-out shorebreak," with another surfer taking off in the "well-shaped slow lineup" of the wave behind. Normal afternoon seabreeze is blowing offshore. [Bob Barada]

El Capitan. (1) Beach surf. (2) Point surf. Size today about 2 feet. Note how lines already coming in at an angle must bend far around to fit contour of point. Swells so "stretched" lose much of their size. Light spots in foreground are patches of kelp. On land: (A) Highway 101. (B) Parking lot.

EL CAPITAN BEACH STATE PARK—There are two distinct surfing areas.

- POINT SURF—The long hollow right slide on the east side of the point comes up only on a strong winter swell and seldom reaches six feet. At high tide surf under four feet breaks too close to the large sharp boulders lining this side of the point; but if enough sand is present you can ride here at low tide, and it is reported that even one-foot waves are hollow and hard-breaking for their size. Sea breeze blows somewhat offshore.

- BEACH SURF—The more usual place to ride is the beach in front of the parking lot. It takes most swells, with peaky wind swells— common in spring—being best. Beach upcoast, in front of privately owned land, offers similar waves. Area is protected from wind chop by kelp outside.

Park is run by State Division of Beaches and Parks. Lifeguards in summer 10 AM to 6 PM. Parking costs 50 cents. No camping. Location: on Highway 101, 17 miles west of Santa Barbara.

Richard Roche cuts back into a clean green wall at EL CAPITAN point.
[Alexander "Skipper" Newton]

CAT CANYON (EDWARDS RANCH)—Right-slide point takes west swell. Rocks protrude above water level in middle of break when surf is 3 feet; at this size short slow rides are available inside. Larger surf may be faster and rides quite long. Point is located 2 miles east of El Capitan in front of private land marked with anti-trespassing signs.

(1) Cat Canyon. On land: (A) Railroad track. (B) Highway 101.

Bobby Hazard on a small wave at EL CAPITAN point. [Gary Connelly]

NAPLES—There are two distinct breaks.

- NAPLES REEF is a shoal shown on U.S. Coast and Geodetic Survey maps as being nine-tenths of a mile from shore and 2½ fathoms (15 feet) deep. Thick peaks appear here during strong winter swells; they must be 10-12 feet to break at all and probably can reach 20.
- NAPLES BEACH—During smaller swells good peaks break along a mile of coastline located inshore from Naples Reef.

Tiny village of Naples is 13 miles west of Santa Barbara and 4 miles east of El Capitan.

Naples. Surf about 4-5 feet along Naples Beach. Naples Reef is not breaking; if it were, white water would be seen in lower right corner. Railroad track (complete with freight train) is between Highway 101 and coast.

(1) The Dunes. Fun-surf today. (2) Devereux's. Messy—breaking too near the rocks. (3) Mushroom House. "Inside Mushroom" is barely breaking. (4) Isla Vista. Hardly better. (A) Storke Road. (B) El Colegio Road. (C) Santa Barbara campus of University of California. (D) Devereux's Ranch School.

SAND BEACH (THE DUNES), which is actually the west side of Coal Oil Point, has better-than-average beach surf on a peaky west swell. Since Devereux's Ranch School nearby is private, surfers must walk or paddle ⅔ mile west from Mushroom House (see next page).

DEVEREUX'S (COAL OIL POINT)—Strong winter swell produces a fast hollow right slide on the east side of the point. Takeoff is over reefs east of point. Waves under five feet are usually sloppy, and rocks in the break are then a hazard; surf size can pass ten feet. Most convenient access would be from Devereux's Ranch School at corner of Storke and El Colegio Roads in Isla Vista, but owners of private property frown on trespassers. Legal access is by walking or paddling ⅓ mile west from Mushroom House (see next page).

MUSHROOM HOUSE—There are two breaks.

- OUTSIDE MUSHROOM—In front of the top-heavy modern home which gives this spot its name, a reef 300 yards out makes thick soupy waves that die away before reaching shore. Takes medium-sized winter swell (5 feet) to break, can reach 8-10. Rights and lefts.
- INSIDE MUSHROOM—Beach break nearer shore ridable to 3 or 4 feet. Waves are usually flat and slow, so area is a good learning spot. Beware of occasional rocks sticking up here and there.

The Mushroom House is located at the west end of Camino de la Playa in Isla Vista.

ISLA VISTA—Average beach surf on any west swell; best when swell is peaky. Waves over 5 or 6 feet wall up and crash. Location: 1 mile west of Goleta. El Colegio Road parallels the coast and several streets lead off to the beach. Public ramp descends cliff at foot of El Embarcadero.

Glenn Merrfield at "The Poles," CAMPUS BEACH. [Dewey Schurman]

Campus Beach. (1) The Point. Note the rocks. (2) The Poles. (3) Inside. Kelp patches clearly visible outside. (A) University of California at Santa Barbara. (B) Santa Barbara Airport. (C) Goleta Slough.

CAMPUS BEACH (GOLETA POINT, COLLEGE POINT)—Lines wind around point forming good waves in three areas.

- THE POINT—Steep peak takeoffs are followed by hard-breaking tubular rights which may section because of submerged reefs. Strong winter swells best. Higher tides preferred. Ridable at any size; largest surf to be expected is 8 feet. Lefts possible when surf is small.
- THE POLES—Waves peak up again 300 yards inside the point near four poles sticking out of the water. Lefts and rights, with latter longer. Occasional good shape in this beach-type surf. Spot favors peakier winter swells and is better at lower tides. Ridable to 8 feet.
- INSIDE—Occasionally there are right-slide point-type waves still farther inside. The best size is 3-4 feet, for smaller waves are powerless and larger ones peel off too fast to make.

Area poor on south swells; those that can get past the offshore islands break along the whole point at once. Beach is sandy except at point, where large rocks are a hazard to boards. Offshore winds frequent, but area becomes blown out if wind persists. Occasional kelp.

Located 8 miles west of Santa Barbara on the campus of the University of California, the beach offers feminine attractions. Visitor parking permit sometimes available from campus police who enforce parking regulations. Lifeguard on duty during warmer months if school is in session. No camping; try Refugio or leech off surfy friends attending college.

The lineup at CAMPUS BEACH. [Dewey Schurman]

SANTA BARBARA—CARPINTERIA AREA

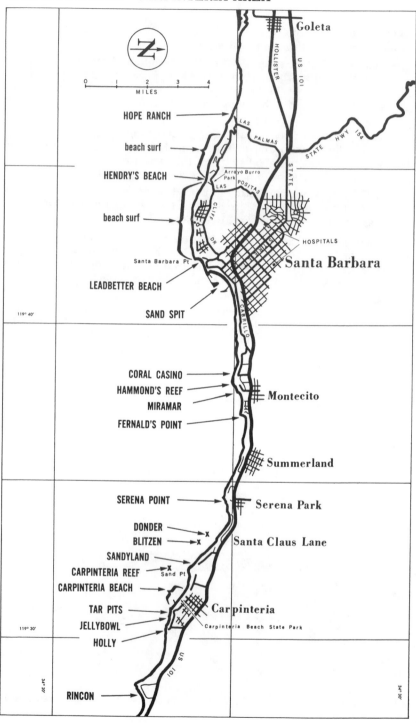

SANTA BARBARA-CARPINTERIA AREA

The surf in this area comes up primarily in winter or on west wind swells, for the offshore islands effectively block most of the swells from the south. Towns from north to south are Santa Barbara, Montecito, Summerland, and Carpinteria. The only campground in the area is at Carpinteria Beach State Park.

HOPE RANCH—Good beach break takes winter swell or local wind swell. Access road is open only to residents and their guests; trespassing is prevented by gatekeeper. Location: 4 miles west of Santa Barbara. Beach surf on either side of Hope Ranch is also ridable but steep cliffs prevent easy access.

A glassy day at HOPE RANCH. The surfer is kicking out at the end of his ride. [Gary Connelly]

Hendry's Beach. (1) North Point. (2) The Pit. The Pendulum lies just to the right of the picture. (A) Cliff Drive. (B) Las Positas Road.

HENDRY'S BEACH. In the foreground is the Pit. The point behind is the Pendulum.
[Ken Stovall]

HENDRY'S BEACH (ARROYO BURRO BEACH STATE PARK)—There are three more or less distinct areas.

- THE PIT—Directly in front of parking lot the waves are usually small and poorly shaped. The shore and bottom are dotted with rocks. In summer a misery cloud of damp fog settles here even when nearby beaches are sunny, further justifying the name the locals have bestowed on their surfing hole.
- THE PENDULUM (MESA LANE)—An even poorer break one-quarter mile south of the Pit.
- NORTH POINT—Peak one-third mile north of the Pit. Many rocks.

The entire area is best during west wind swells most common in spring and early summer.

Park is operated by Santa Barbara County. Lifeguard 10 AM to 6 PM in warmer months. Surfing is allowed at all hours though surfboard area may be restricted to protect swimmers.

From main part of Santa Barbara go west on Cliff Drive and descend into the Pit ⅓ mile west of Las Positas Road, which connects with Highway 101.

Shaun Claffey gives this typical HENDRY'S BEACH wave more than it deserves.
[Gary Connelly]

Leadbetter Beach. Surf is slow here because Santa Barbara Point is so pronounced. Check beach surf to left below 150-foot cliffs.

LEADBETTER BEACH—Several reefs in lee of Santa Barbara Point produce thickish waves on any swell, with west best. Observant surfers will find occasional short hot lineups mixed in with the mush. Ridable from 2 to 8 feet. Rarely blown out. Lifeguard ¼ mile east, 10 AM to 5 PM in summer. Fire pits. Food in nearby Santa Barbara. Location: just west of harbor.

LEADBETTER BEACH from the cliff above. [Ken Stovall]

(1) The Sand Spit. Swells can be seen moving in toward breakwater and breaking on sand spit. Size about 9 inches. (A) Highway 101. Panorama: Santa Barbara harbor and city.

SAND SPIT—Swells from any direction bend around Santa Barbara harbor breakwater and create exceedingly hollow waves when they reach the sand spit. Fast takeoffs frequently followed by inside-the-tube rides if surf is big enough. When surf is 10 feet at other good spots it might be 4 feet here. Good only at lower tides; may not break at all when tide is high unless swell is huge. Usual sea breeze blows offshore. Pilings and other garbage sticking out of water are hazards. Also skeg occasionally hits shallow sandbar, resulting in annoying wipeout. Law which prohibits surfing here is now enforced strictly by Santa Barbara City Harbormaster, and planned additions to harbor will probably destroy the surf in near future.

Springtime at HAMMOND'S REEF. The birds head north, while Kemp Aaberg and Renny Yater fly south into a long wall. [Dick Perry]

(1) Coral Casino. (2) Hammond's Reef. (3) Miramar. (4) Fernald's Point. (5) Serena Point. (A) Montecito. (B) Summerland. (C) Highway 101.

CORAL CASINO (BILTMORE HOTEL) Some winter swells produce usually unmakable peaks near the hotel. Size can reach 12 feet. Location: in Montecito, 3 miles east of Santa Barbara, at foot of Olive Mill Road.

HAMMOND'S REEF—Waves peak up quickly and mysteriously, offering well-shaped fast rights and occasional lefts. Usually hollow and hard-breaking. Good from 3 to 15 feet; surf over 8 feet or so breaks on reef farther out to sea, so beware the outside set! Breaks best but inconsistently on winter swells. Occasionally big south swells sneak in and make lefts superior to the rights. Medium-high tides preferred; at lower tides waves become crumbly and hazardous rocks are exposed. Unlike many Santa Barbara County surfing areas this spot has little kelp to protect it from onshore winds. Currents strong when surf is big, at which time paddling out may be difficult. The break is in front of the Hammond Estate, which is private property: no trespassing or loitering above high-tide line. Access, however, is relatively uncomplicated: walk or paddle ⅓ mile east from Biltmore area or west from Miramar area.

MIRAMAR HOTEL—Winter swell brings up right slide ridable to eight feet. Waves often somewhat thick. Popular with local gremmies. Public access at foot of Eucalyptus Lane in Montecito, 4 miles east of Santa Barbara. Turn off Highway 101 at San Ysidro Road.

FERNALD'S POINT (SHARK COVE)—There are two spots.
- Right slide point surf inside is usually small and may be marred by backwash from twin jetties.
- Peak outside point can get hollow. Mostly rights, a few short lefts. Rarely over 6 feet.

Area breaks on any swell but not consistently; west swell best. Private property; no parking (owners call police). Nearest public beach access is at Miramar Hotel, ⅔ mile west.

FERNALD'S POINT from Highway 101. [Bob Cooper]

Serena Point. (1) Outer Point. (2) Peak break. (3) Inner Point.

SERENA POINT—Potentially breaks on swells from any direction but is inconsistent. Winter swell is voted most likely to succeed. There are actually two points half a mile apart (both rights), with a peak break in between. Has been surfed at 10 feet. Entire area is fronted by private property. No parking or trespassing; owners call police. Location: 3 miles west of Carpinteria.

DONDER and **BLITZEN**—Two peak breaks which have been spotted during a huge west swell in front of Santa Claus Lane, a tiny community located 2 miles above Carpinteria.

SANDYLAND—Average quality beach break on west side of Sand Point takes most swells with peaky ones best. This is a private residential area which is patrolled; no trespassing. Location: 1 mile above Carpinteria.

CARPINTERIA REEF—Peaks break in a confused pattern over reefs extending half a mile or more to sea just east of Sand Point. Takes winter swell and reaches 15 feet. Best rides are rights. In places the reefs are very shallow, so that surfing during smaller swells can be dangerous. In larger surf the shoulder of the wave is in deeper water and hence may be safer. Area is unprotected from wind. Paddle out from west end of Carpinteria Beach.

Carpinteria. (1) Municipal Beach. (2) State Beach. Tar Pits out of sight at right. (A) Highway 101.

CARPINTERIA BEACH—Municipal beach offers waves similar to those in adjoining state park.

CARPINTERIA BEACH STATE PARK—Typical beach break is best on small peaky west swell; surf over 4 or 5 feet tends to wall up and crash. However, a peak north of the Carpinteria Pier offers a good takeoff at 6-8 feet, and still larger surf breaks 300-400 yards out on a reef south of the pier. Area is best at medium to high tides. Surfers are usually asked to stay on south side of pier. Lifeguards 8 AM to 7 PM daily. Parking costs 50 cents. Camping costs $1 per car; party must include "responsible adult." Dressing rooms, fire pits, snack bar. Supplies in nearby Carpinteria.

TAR PITS—Easy beach-type peak breaks over slate bottom. Summer swell preferred. Lefts better than rights. Blows out fairly easily. In front of private property ¼ mile below Carpinteria pier.

JELLY BOWL—A short small mediocre right slide. Private property. Location: ½ mile below Carpinteria pier.

CARPINTERIA PIER. [David Stern]

Merv Larson, CARPINTERIA BEACH. [Toni Larson]

Merv Larson sprays foam with his head and right hand while Mr. Huge watches impassively.
CARPINTERIA BEACH. [Toni Larson]

HOLLY during a big west-southwest swell. [David Stern]

HOLLY—Waves break over reefs just east of bend in coastline not pronounced enough to call a point. Rights are commoner than lefts. Most rides are either slow or encounter unmakable sections or both. Area takes any swell. Location: 1 mile below Carpinteria. Cliffs prevent direct access.

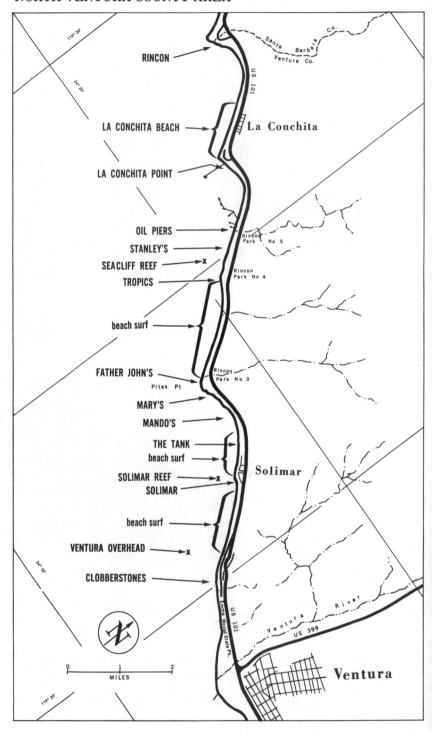

RINCON

LA CONCHITA BEACH

La Conchita

LA CONCHITA POINT

OIL PIERS

STANLEY'S

SEACLIFF REEF

TROPICS

beach surf

FATHER JOHN'S

Pitas Pt

MARY'S

MANDO'S

THE TANK

beach surf

SOLIMAR REEF

Solimar

SOLIMAR

beach surf

VENTURA OVERHEAD

CLOBBERSTONES

Rincon Park No 5

Rincon Park No 4

Rincon Park No 3

US 101

US 399

Ventura River

Emma Wood State Pk.

Ventura

Santa Barbara Co.
Ventura Co.

0   1   2
MILES

NORTH VENTURA COUNTY AREA

Highway 101 runs right along the shore; hence surf conditions speak for themselves. The entire coastline is surfable, with several point breaks and reef breaks interspersed with plenty of frequently glassy beach surf. Nearest large towns are Carpinteria to north and Ventura to south. Camping is allowed at Rincon Parks Numbers 3, 4, and 5, located 7, 9, and 10 miles above Ventura respectively, and at Emma Wood Beach State Park, 3 miles above Ventura.

A shining afternoon and ten-foot waves at RINCON. This photograph taken in 1947 shows a tantalizing absence of people. [Joe Quigg]

A perfect day at Rincon. Surf 3-4 feet. (1) First Point. Arrow points at surfers sitting farther inside than they should. (2) Second Point. If Rincon Bombora were breaking, it would be out of sight off right corner of photo.

RINCON (RINCON DEL MAR, SANTA BARBARA COUNTY LINE)—Long lines wind around point forming three basic breaks.

- FIRST POINT provides steep takeoff which develops into beautiful hollow nearly perfect right lineup for as far as 400 yards. Though fast, waves permit much turning and nose-riding when small (2-7 feet); locked-in-the-tube rides are frequent. Larger surf (up to 15 feet), still faster and harder-breaking, usually requires trimming for maximum speed but turning is possible sometimes. Breaks year round, but summer waves are mushy and hard to make, hardly resembling quality winter surf. Peaky after-storm surf is small and poor here. Best at low-to-medium tides, when waves are challenging and break hardest; higher tides make them fatter and somewhat bumpy because of backwash from the outer point. At very low tides, bowl after takeoff often becomes a long unmakable section.

- SECOND POINT (OUTER POINT, INDICATOR) breaks in a peak a couple feet larger than inside. Lefts preferred in summer, rights in winter. High tide best. Must be 3 or 4 feet to be worth riding, and not good till 6 feet or bigger. Usual ride is 100-200 yards, but on freak waves surfers have ridden full length of point from here (½ mile).

- RINCON BOMBORA—A reef ⅓ mile or more from shore which sometimes caps over when surf pushes 15 feet.

Prevailing sea breeze blows along the shore, so that surf doesn't usually blow out. Most of beach is sandy, but at higher tides huge boulders next to highway are dangerous both to boards and to careless surfers. Smaller and sharper rocks extending from below mean high tide line far out into water all along beach are a minor hazard but a major nuisance —small dings and cut feet common. Rips relatively infrequent, but strong downcast current during moderate or large swells can carry surfers in front of aforementioned boulders; if this happens, extreme caution may be necessary to leave water safely.

Location: at Santa Barbara-Ventura county line, 13 miles north of Ventura, 14 miles south of Santa Barbara. Parking alongside highway. Market 2 miles south near highway, many cafes and markets 4 miles north in Carpinteria. Access from Highway 101 is public, but homes lining point are private. No camping here; camping for $1 per car per night 4 miles north at Carpinteria Beach State Park—if one member of party is 21 or over and party is deemed "responsible." Camping also at Rincon Parks Numbers 3, 4, and 5, located 3 to 7 miles south.

Lance Carson, RINCON. ". . . locked-in-the-tube rides frequent . . ." [Leroy Grannis]

This classic shot was taken at RINCON on January 10, 1953. Thinking he had a moment to spare Matt Kivlin made a cutback, as the change in the angle of his board wake reveals. Realizing his mistake he trimmed up, but he was too late. The wave sectioned in front before he could get by. [Joe Quigg]

Mickey Dora relaxes on a perfectly shaped shoulder at RINCON as a swimmer ducks under an inshore wave. [Leroy Grannis]

A natural wonder: hot tubes through cold water. Ken Kesson, RINCON. [John Edwards]

(1) La Conchita Beach. (2) La Conchita Point. Uneven white-water line here indicates that surf is very sectiony, as is usual when size is 3 feet. Note jetty inside (A).

LA CONCHITA BEACH—Fair beach surf north of northernmost oil pier, 2 miles below Rincon.

LA CONCHITA POINT (MUSSEL SHOALS)—Long point lined with granite boulders makes mostly mush when swell is weak, with rights and some lefts. On big north swell, however, peak near pier is followed by long well-shaped right lineup sometimes makable for a quarter-mile. At any but low tides the rocks on shore and in the water are rough on boards. Location: 2½ miles south of Rincon, just south of northernmost oil pier (the one with the island at the end).

(1) The Oil Piers. (2) Stanley's. Surf 2-3 feet. Much kelp in foreground.

THE OIL PIERS—Small peaks form on sand bars created by piers. Rides usually short but fast, with good nose-rides in both directions. Lefts and rights. Breaks hard, wipeouts frequent. Takes most swells, but peaky wind swells best. Often lines up and crashes at 4 feet, but sometimes ridable to 8. Doesn't blow out easily. Beach and bottom both sandy. Pier seldom an obstacle. South oil pier can be shot at low tide, but cross-bars at chest height add horizontal obstacles to the usual vertical ones. Location: 3½ miles south of Rincon.

STANLEY'S (RINCON PARK NO. 5)—Smooth peak: lefts and rights. Sand bottom. Takes most swells, west-southwest best. County park has restrooms, stoves, picnic tables; camping costs $1 per car per night. Best spot to surf is just south of park in front of restaurant for which spot is named.

Bob "Porkchop" Barron buries his head in the sea at the OIL PIERS. [Dale "Tuna" Davis]

Bill Cleary takes time off from writing at the OIL PIERS. [Co Rentmeester]

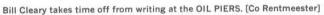

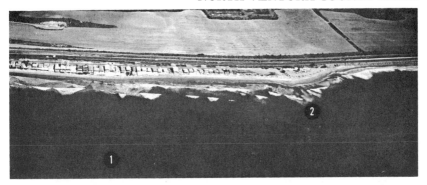

(1) Where white-water would appear if Seacliff Reef were breaking. (2) Tropics. Surf about 3 feet. Stanley's just out of sight at left. Highway 101 runs along coast.

SEACLIFF REEF—Peak builds 300 yards offshore, becomes very steep and often holds up without breaking. Takes big strong winter swell. Location: ¼ mile below Stanley's.

TROPICS (RINCON PARK NO. 4, HOBSON PARK)—Peaks break in front of small point decorated by a few palm trees. Rights predominate in winter, lefts in summer. Surf frequently mushy, but lower tide makes waves hollow out. Winter surf more consistent. Seldom crowded, lots of room. Ventura County provides park with restrooms, stoves, fireplaces; camping costs $1 per car per night. Location: 5 miles south of Rincon, 9 miles north of Ventura.

BEACH SURF between Tropics and Pitas Point is often good, especially near Tropics.

Greg Liddle, STANLEY'S. The thin glassy waves pictured on these two pages are typical of the surf found at most of the straight sandy beaches between Ventura and Point Conception. Surfers from "down south" are often surprised at this, for their beach break waves are usually thicker, more uneven, and less smooth.   [Kent Potvin]

Pitas Point. (1) Father John's. (2) Mary's. (3) Mando's. (4) The Tank. Shallow bottom is outlined as a lighter grayish area. Between Mary's and Father John's you can see "bad" kelp all along the white-water line. Contrast with photo on page 63 showing "good" kelp growing in large patches much farther from shore and thus protecting the Oil Piers from wind chop.

PITAS POINT—The longest point in Southern California offers three separate spots.

- FATHER JOHN'S (RINCON PARK No. 3)—Left breaks at the west end of the point on a south swell. Camping is allowed here for $1 per car per night.

- MARY'S—Outer part of point produces fast well-shaped but sometimes unmakable rights on strong winter swells; smaller waves break too close to rocks. Private homes line this part of beach.

- MANDO'S—Surf farther inside is most often ridden. Long lines moving in past the mile-long point give up their strength, so that takeoffs over reefs are slow; and though lineups are well-shaped and sometimes even unmakable, they still feel slow. Rights and lefts available, with rights commoner. Small rocks ding boards and surfers. Area takes all swells, but is rarely over 5 feet. Usually glassy, being in lee of point when westerlies blow. Waves break a little harder at medium-to-high tide. This is one of the best learning spots on the coast, due to gentle characteristics of waves, uncrowded conditions, and large space in which people can spread out. Public access from highway at large gap between houses at east end of point is apparently unrestricted.

Area is located 5½ miles north of Ventura.

THE TANK—All of beach between Mando's and Solimar is surfable, but peaks are frequently best in front of small tank between Highway 101 and beach. Local wind swell preferred. Does not blow out easily.

Solimar. (1) Where reef breaks when swell is larger. (2) Inside. The Tank is out of sight at left, the Overhead out of sight at right.

SOLIMAR   There are two breaks.

- SOLIMAR REEF: Very fast sucking-out peak takeoff 300 yards off outer part of point is followed by short steep fast ride before wave backs off and dies away. High tide a must; low tide exposes dangerously shallow rocks on which wave breaks. South swell best, but any large enough swell breaks.

- INSIDE SOLIMAR: Lines bend around small point and peak up over reefs into thick rather mushy waves, but soup is powerless and large sections are makable. Some lefts, more often rights. Rocks a hazard.

Location: 4 miles above Ventura.

BEACH SURF found between Solimar and the Overhead is fair. Peaks in front of two small canyons sometimes resembles surf at the Tank and Stanley's.

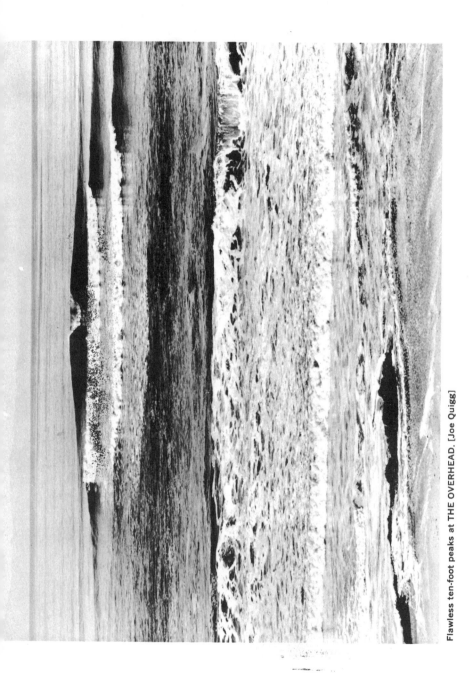

Flawless ten-foot peaks at THE OVERHEAD. [Joe Quigg]

Two surfers head right and three more left on a glassy OVERHEAD wave. [Frank Zenk]

VENTURA OVERHEAD (EMMA WOOD BEACH STATE PARK) There are four distinct spots.

- THE OVERHEAD—Strong swells create classic peaks on reefs one-quarter to one-half mile from shore, in front of highway overpass. Winter swells make best surf, though big south swells are sometimes ridable. Waves begin to cap over at 4 or 5 feet if tide is low but do not appear well-shaped below 6 or 7. At 8 to 15 feet takeoff is straight-up-and-down, and peak throws out huge volume of water, breaking very hard. Takeoff in peak is essential; paddling into waves on the shoulder leads either to not catching the wave or to excruciating wipeout, with long swim for board in cold and treacherous waters. Quality of lineup after takeoff improves with wave size. Rides up to one-third mile in length are possible. Surf over 15 feet sometimes breaks with less shape on outside reefs. Lower tides help smaller surf (up to 8 or 10 feet) become well-shaped, while larger surf can break well at all tides. Any wind except directly offshore will make area choppy. Shorebreak is wild, especially at higher tides, when it can smash a lost board into rocks lining the beach. Strong rip south of peak aids in paddling out; lost boards will often be found here. Beware the outside set!
- TIDE HOLE—At low tide if the outer reefs are barely breaking, wave may peak with better shape slightly north and half as far out to sea.
- OVERHEAD SHOREBREAK—South swell makes shorebreak ridable. Good takeoffs and very fast hollow waves, with lefts usually longer and better shaped than rights. Reaches 6-7 feet.
- CLOBBERSTONES—Right slides break all along the beach between the Overhead and the Ventura River Mouth. Waves are rarely makable and beach is very rocky, as name implies.

Location: 3 miles north of Ventura, with entrance to park being ⅓ mile past the highway overhead bridge. Fire pits. Rest rooms. Food in Ventura. Lifeguard on duty in summer (but surf is on duty in winter).

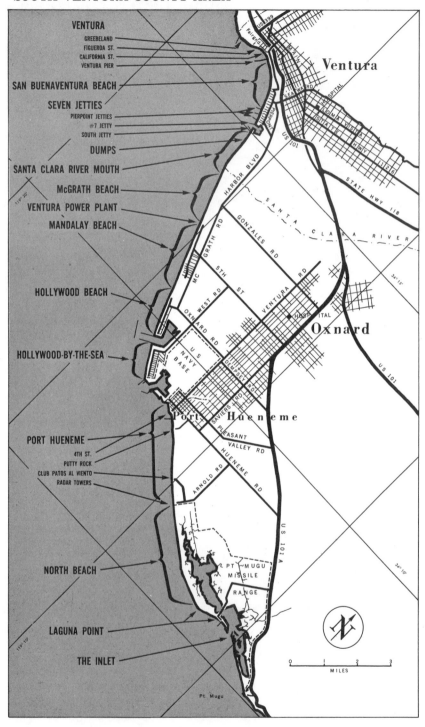

VENTURA
GREEBELAND
FIGUEROA ST.
CALIFORNIA ST.
VENTURA PIER

SAN BUENAVENTURA BEACH

SEVEN JETTIES
PIERPOINT JETTIES
#7 JETTY
SOUTH JETTY

DUMPS

SANTA CLARA RIVER MOUTH

McGRATH BEACH

VENTURA POWER PLANT

MANDALAY BEACH

HOLLYWOOD BEACH

HOLLYWOOD-BY-THE-SEA

PORT HUENEME
4TH ST.
PUTTY ROCK
CLUB PATOS AL VIENTO
RADAR TOWERS

NORTH BEACH

LAGUNA POINT

THE INLET

Ventura

Oxnard

Port Hueneme

Pt. Mugu

0   1   2   3
MILES

SOUTH VENTURA COUNTY AREA

The entire coastline from Ventura to Point Mugu (with few exceptions) is very surfable and yet is rarely ridden. Furthermore, if there is any kind of swell running it is almost certain that somewhere in this area there will be ridable waves unless everything is blown out. For people seeking their own private wave, exploring these beaches can be very rewarding. It will be many years before the region becomes overcrowded with surfers.

There are no campgrounds in the area at present, though the future calls for such facilities at McGrath Beach State Park, 4 miles south of Ventura on Harbor Avenue. Towns include Ventura, Oxnard (inland) and Port Hueneme.

The largest wave in the world? As some persons on the VENTURA PIER walk by seemingly unconcerned, one man points and stares immobilized at the fantastic apparition which minutes later swept over the entire city of Ventura. Its height has been estimated at over 250 feet. This is the only known photograph. For further details see page 74. [Merrill Allyn]

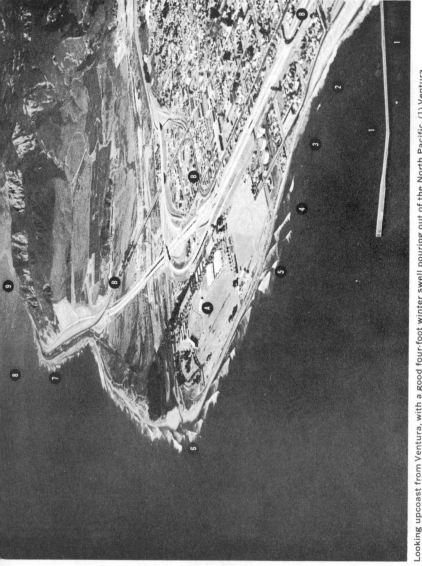

Looking upcoast from Ventura, with a good four-foot winter swell pouring out of the North Pacific. (1) Ventura Pier. (2) California Street. (3) Oak Street. (4) Palm Street. Note surfwagons parked here. (5) Figueroa Street. (6) Greebeland, with Ventura River entering ocean just beyond. (7) Clobberstones. (8) Ventura Overhead (not breaking). (9) Solimar. (10) Pitas Point. (A) Ventura Fairground. (B) Highway 101.

Ventura. (1) Greebeland. Note drainpipe sticking out into the white-water. (2) California Street area; from left: Figueroa, Palm, Oak and California Streets. (3) Ventura Pier. (4) San Buenaventura Beach. Highway 101 is shown as a finished freeway south of California Street; farther north it is still under construction.

VENTURA—Point extends nearly a mile from Ventura River Mouth to Ventura Pier and has ridable waves all along, so that there is lots of room for many surfers. While any place is good, surfers single out:

- GREEBELAND (VENTURA COUNTY FAIRGROUND, BALL-PARK, STABLES, PIPE, SEWER, VENTURA RIVER MOUTH)— Summer swell produces rather powerless waves with lefts and rights possible, but winter swell makes rights long and well-shaped when 6 feet or more. Ridable from 3 feet up. Pipe extending into water is a potential hazard. Access through fairground main gate.
- CALIFORNIA, OAK, PALM, FIGUEROA STREETS—In this area smaller swells from any direction produce peaks in several places; much turning is possible on well-shaped but seldom fast waves. Sometimes surf allows long rides involving several complete changes of direction—as at San Onofre or Waikiki. Inside breaks permit good nose-rides. When surf is larger lefts disappear and long right slides are available (400 yards); but strong downcoast current then can carry boards and surfers to pier, which is dangerous. Underwater pipe extending seaward at Figueroa Street is a hazard to riders at low tide, rocks and seawall at water's edge a hazard to boards at high tide.

- VENTURA PIER—South side of pier produces good small surf on some west swells. Lefts are better. In larger swells (8 feet or more) peaks on either side are ridable but north peak is dangerous because of downcoast drift which may carry surfer under pier. Waves have broken beyond end of pier at heights up to 20 feet. And sometimes there are thick fog banks off the end of the pier, such as the one in the photo on Page 71, which we included in the guidebook just for fun.

Area blows out at slightest provocation. Cafes and markets on Meta Avenue two blocks inland; snack bar and restaurant on pier.

SAN BUENAVENTURA BEACH STATE PARK—Small beach surf of mediocre quality. Surfing restricted when beach is crowded. Parking costs 50 cents. Lifeguards 8 AM to 5 PM in summer; ranger in residence year round. Dressing rooms, fire pits on beach; restaurant and snack stand on pier. Location: just south of Ventura Pier in Ventura.

Maybe not the largest in the world, but a good-sized comber for the VENTURA PIER.
[Frank Zenk]

The Seven Jetties. (1) Two of the three Pierpont Jetties. (2) Number Seven Jetty. (3) South Jetty. The Dumps lies just to the right of the picture, north of where the Santa Clara River (A) reaches the ocean. (B) Ventura Marina. (C) Highway 101 as it leaves Ventura and turns inland towards Oxnard. (D) Harbor Avenue. (E) Pierpont Avenue.

THE SEVEN JETTIES—There are five jetties now; four more are planned. At some point, presumably, there will be seven.

- PIERPONT JETTIES—The three northerly jetties stick straight out from the beach, improving somewhat the otherwise ordinary beach surf by creating sandbars. Area takes all swells, but winter surf becomes larger.

- NUMBER SEVEN JETTY (PEPPERMINT WEDGE NORTH)— North jetty of Ventura Marina points downcoast, deflecting waves coming straight in to beach. First wave of set is not ridden; but as second wave approaches, the backwash from the first moves across it to make a wedge-like peak considerably higher than the rest of the wave. Takeoff in this peak is very steep and fast. Only lefts are possible. Ridable from 4-12 feet; smaller surf is ordinary beach break, while larger surf closes out. Jetty is very grave danger to both surfers and boards. Wild currents and rips abound.

- SOUTH JETTY—At present fast lefts break off the end of the south jetty of the Ventura Marina, but dredging will probably kill them.

Area breaks best on a wind swell; it also breaks well on a medium-sized west or north swell. In winter waves here can reach twenty feet in height. Unridable at this size, they are remarkable to watch while standing safely on shore. Jetties are located in southern Ventura; leave Highway 101 at Seaward Avenue and drive south on Pierpont Avenue. Food and supplies near freeway turn-off now, in future also at Ventura Marina.

Ken Tilton escapes the pounding ferocity of a thick wedge at NUMBER SEVEN JETTY.
[Walt Phillips]

This "closeup" of the Ventura Power Plant was shot about 20 seconds before the picture on the facing page. As careful comparison of the two will reveal, white water generated by the outermost wave in this photo can still be seen in the other one, though more faintly.

THE DUMPS (SANTA CLARA RIVER MOUTH)—Beach surf good on any swell and best in winter. Sometimes Santa Clara River deposits sandbar on which peaks up to 15 feet and more break and are ridable if you can paddle out to them. Location: just south of Ventura Marina.

McGRATH BEACH STATE PARK—Here three miles of good beach surf have been preserved for the public by state acquisition of the land. Facilities, including campsites, are planned for the near future. Location: just south of Santa Clara River on Harbor Avenue.

Mandalay Beach. Surf all along is 3-5 feet. (1) Ventura Power Plant. (A) Harbor Avenue. (B) West Fifth Street, which leads straight to Oxnard, far in background. (C) Mandalay Beach Road.

VENTURA POWER PLANT (STEAM PLANT)—Beach surf usually indistinguishable from that of rest of Mandalay Beach to south, although water flowing out of power plant sometimes creates a good sandbar. Tired surfers can relax in the warm water emitted here. Location: north end of Mandalay Beach Road.

MANDALAY BEACH (OXNARD SHORES)—Two miles of good beach surf comes up on most swells, with winter more consistent and peaky swells best. Best size is 3-7 feet; smaller surf often breaks near shore or walls up too much. Medium tide preferred. Area blown out by south and west winds but good on glassy mornings. Surf is never crowded. Location: 6 miles south of Ventura. To get there from Oxnard drive due west on Fifth Street to Mandalay Beach Road, which runs along the shore.

Ventura County's vacant waves. Top: STEAM PLANT [Greg Liddle]. Bottom: NUMBER SEVEN JETTY [Walt Phillips]. Opposite page top: HOLLYWOOD-BY-THE-SEA [David Stern]. Middle: HOLLYWOOD-BY-THE-SEA [Richard Vincent]. Bottom: NUMBER SEVEN JETTY [Eric Arneson].

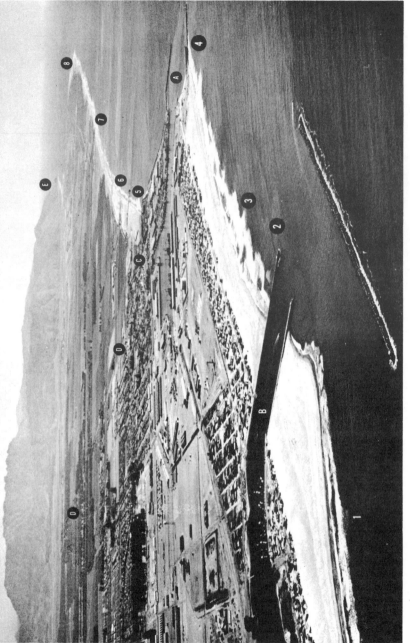

(1) Hollywood Beach, which continues northward for a mile. Offshore breakwater diminishes size of surf behind it. (2-4) Hollywood-by-the-Sea: (2) North Jetty. (3) Hollywood Bowl. (4) Washing Machine. (5-7) Port Hueneme: (5) Fourth Street. (6) Putty Rock. (7) Club Patos al Viento and Radar Towers. (8) Laguna Point, on the Point Mugu Missile Range. Surf today is about 3-4 feet at Hollywood-by-the-Sea and on the missile range, but the west swell misses Port Hueneme. (A) Port Hueneme Harbor. (B) Oxnard Harbor. (C) City of Port Hueneme. (D) Hueneme Road. (E) Point Mugu.

HOLLYWOOD BEACH—One mile of beach break generally resembles that of Oxnard Shores. Jetties and breakwater at south end keep out part of the swell, so that waves here will be smaller and perhaps ridable when breaks to north are closed out. Also they protect the entire area somewhat from certain south winds. Location: 8 miles south of Ventura. To reach this beach follow Oxnard Road to the ocean.

HOLLYWOOD-BY-THE-SEA (SILVER STRAND)—Excellent beach break along one mile of beach between two harbors, with lines that build over sandbars into strong well-shaped peaks on larger swells (over 6 feet) and offering rides in both directions. On smaller swells average two-way beach surf is available. Consistently over 4 feet in winter and occasionally up to 15. Large waves break very hard and are very hollow. When surf is this big you can paddle out in the harbor channels. Peaks form all along the beach, so that area can accommodate many surfers without becoming overcrowded. Spots singled out are:

- NORTH JETTY—Best on west swell.

- HOLLYWOOD BOWL—Hollow peak in middle of beach.

- WASHING MACHINE—Very hard-breaking peak near south jetty. Lefts usually longer and better-shaped than rights; rides near jetty are very dangerous because it sticks out at an angle. Spot is named for what wipeouts feel like being in. Pure confusion paddling out.

Area is a good "mysto-spot" because it may break big when other places are flat. Blown out early and easily by any west and some south winds. Area has wide sandy beach with much broken glass. Only ocean hazards are jetties and rough water in big surf; strong rips near jetties. Rest rooms on sand 3 blocks from south end of beach. Cafe near there too; market near north end a block inland. Lifeguard only in summer and only at south end of beach.

PORT HUENEME—Surf along the 2½ miles of beach between Port Hueneme Harbor and Point Mugu Missile Range is rarely ridden because the area lies off the surfers' main drag (Highway 101). As a whole the area takes a south swell well, and the eastern portion also breaks on some west swells. Most north swells seem to miss it. Waves 3-4 feet high peak on sandbars paralleling the beach 50-75 yards from shore; smaller surf breaks right on the sand. To reach the spots turn off Highway 101 five miles south of Oxnard onto Hueneme Road; accessible places, from east to west, are listed on the next page.

- RADAR TOWERS: Turn off Hueneme Road 2 miles west of Highway 101 at Arnold Road and continue 2 miles to its end at the beach. South or west swell.
- CLUB PATOS AL VIENTO—Private dirt road (no trespassing) leads from near end of Arnold Road to the beach. South or west swell.
- PUTTY ROCK (PUMPING PLANT)—Drive 2 miles past Arnold Road on Hueneme Road. At "J" Street, which heads north, turn south onto dirt road and follow concrete riverbed to site of pumping plant. South swell only. Good from 2 to 6 feet.
- FOURTH STREET—Public beach for Port Hueneme with change room, snackwagon, and parking lot. South swell only. Short pier just south has no effect on surf.

John Schommer at "North Jetty," HOLLYWOOD-BY-THE-SEA. [David Stern]

Bob Cooper in his pre-beard days at Putty Rock, PORT HUENEME. [Harold Fred]

POINT MUGU MISSILE RANGE—This area is the site of much defense activity and is therefore quite closed to the public. Our spies, however, reveal the following four places to surf, truly "secret spots":

- NORTH BEACH—Three miles of ridable beach surf on most summer and some winter swells. There are three small jetties near its east end.
- OUTSIDE LAGUNA POINT—Breaks on any swell with south best, must be 4 feet to be ridable, gets up to 12 or more, best at 6-7. Medium-steep peak followed by hollow lineup, either left or right.
- INSIDE LAGUNA POINT—Thin hollow wave breaks near sandy shore, ridable up to 10 feet. Best on southwest swells. Right slide. Long rides possible occasionally.
- THE INLET (MUGU LAGOON)—Waves break farther from shore because of sandbar formed by tidal currents at mouth of lagoon. Takes most swells with summer better. Lefts usually preferred. Best after dredging, which is done periodically.

Note that Point Mugu itself (usually unsurfable) is not on the base but is just south of Mugu Lagoon, where Highway 101 cuts through a rocky ridge. Trespassing is inadvisable. At Trestles (see Page 165) the Marines use rifles, but here your antagonists are armed with Polaris rockets and nuclear submarines.

There are no surfing spots worthy of the name between Point Mugu and County Line. If desperate, try sliding down the sand dunes ½ mile north of Big Sycamore Canyon Pier.

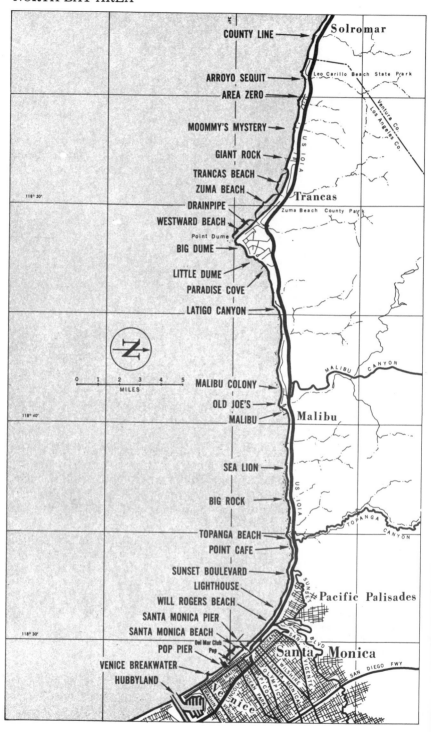

NORTH BAY AREA

The northern part of Santa Monica Bay extends from Point Dume southward to Marina del Rey and includes the towns of Malibu, Santa Monica, Ocean Park and Venice. "North Bay Area" refers to this portion of the coast plus the coast north of Point Dume to just past the Los Angeles-Ventura county line. Only a small percentage of this coastline is surfable, and several of the ridable breaks are in front of privately owned land. Thus the supply of surf is small in relation to the already oppressive and still growing demand, and surfers seeking uncrowded beaches will frequently be disappointed. So if you arrive to find the water swarming with a milling mob remember those vacant waves a few miles farther north in Ventura County.

Doug Nelson drops into a good-sized wave at COUNTY LINE. [Frank Zenk]

County Line. (1) The Point. Surfers scattered along it are waiting hopefully. (2) Beach peaks—not breaking. (3) Estimated location of County Line Bombora. Harrison Reef out of sight at right. Kelp in foreground.

COUNTY LINE (SOLROMAR, LITTLE SYCAMORE CANYON)—On nearly any swell ridable waves break along most of this beach.

- THE POINT—Best place to ride usually is in front of point at north end. On most swells waves have either little shape or many sections. But on west and southwest swells larger than 5 feet a hollow peak develops and is followed by a well-formed lineup for 150-200 yards to the right. Short hot lefts are sometimes possible too.
- THE BEACH—Along the beach farther south, peaks break with good shape, offering 100-yard lefts as well as rights. Watch for them the day after a local storm.
- HARRISON REEF—Half-mile farther south peaks break far out and quickly disintegrate. Reefs exposed at low tide. Rarely ridden.
- COUNTY LINE BOMBORA—In front of the center of the beach and 600 yards from shore a peak breaks and backs off immediately. Must be 10 feet to break. Very steep takeoff, no ride at all.

Area is best at medium tide, for low tide destroys what shape there is, and high tide may create unmakable walls. Usual size range is 3-6 feet; occasionally reaches 12 feet. Late takeoffs best; sitting too far out is a common error because the waves appear steep enough to catch before they actually are. Kelp protects area from light west winds, but south winds bring chop. Sandy beach is lined with small rocks below high tide line near point; point itself is very rocky and boards lost here are assured of dings. Broken glass on beach. Strong currents and rips near Harrison Reef in larger surf.

Location: 1 mile north of Los Angeles-Ventura county line, 27 miles above Santa Monica, 15 miles below Oxnard. Beach is privately owned; at present public is granted free access. Parking on highway. Hamburger stand on point; market, restaurant and gas station across highway.

Richard Roche, COUNTY LINE. Behind him a surfer is paddling into a big mistake.
[Skipper Newton]

The last wave of a small set at ARROYO SEQUIT. [Leroy Grannis]

(1) Arroyo Sequit, crowded as usual. Three-foot wave has just broken next to rock. Surfers' cars can be seen parked along Highway 101, but since this aerial was taken "No Parking" signs have appeared there and lot across street has been opened.

ARROYO SEQUIT (SECOS, LEO CARILLO BEACH STATE PARK)—Peak near rock runs into excellent lineup extending for 150 yards to right, with long nose-rides frequent. Breaks on south and west swells but not north; south swell is more likely to be well-shaped. Usually small waves (2-4 feet), but surfable to 6-8 feet, at which size most swells close out. Lower tides destroy normal (almost perfect) shape; best at medium tide. West sea breeze is strong but blows along the shore, and area is further protected by point and by kelp outside. South wind (infrequent) brings chop. Beach sandy, but small sharp rocks extend into water below mean high tide line. Main hazard is from rocks farther out. At takeoff point surge can force surfer against big rock. More importantly, another rock 10 feet southeast is submerged at higher tides. Other submerged rocks outside and south of big one pose dangers depending on swell and tide. Kelp present outside can become bothersome, especially during critical takeoffs on larger waves from in front of the big rock. Water often unexpectedly cold. More than 6 or 7 surfers makes water feel crowded. Usual summer crowd, 20 to 50.

Location: ⅓ mile south of Los Angeles-Ventura county line, 25 miles above Santa Monica. Lifeguard 10 AM to 6 PM daily in summer, weekends in winter. Parking lot fee is 50 cents; no parking on highway. Snack bars in park. Camping costs $1 per car per night. Additional facilities planned for near future include boat mooring and small pier; we hope they will not injure the surf.

AREA ZERO (POINT NICHOLAS)—Strong lines form an excellent peak just north of partly submerged rocky point, with fast takeoffs and an even faster and hollower left lineup ending in crunching shorebreak. Ridable from 3 to 12 feet; best over 6. Breaks mainly in summer; a few winter swells are ridable if size is over 6 feet. Good at medium to lower tides; walls up at higher tides. Not blown out easily due to heavy kelp outside. Beach and bottom both sandy. Occasional rips and strong currents in larger surf.

Located in front of private beach; access limited to residents and their guests. Los Angeles County ordinance makes trespassing a misdemeanor subject to possible $500 fine and/or 6 months in jail. Law enforced by Malibu Sheriff at request of residents, who are extremely unfriendly and do not hesitate to blow the whistle on uninvited surfers. Even paddling or walking down from Secos (1 mile north) does not guarantee freedom from conflict with property-owners, who claim that retrieving lost board from beach after wipeout constitutes trespassing and have been known to express their conviction by pelting boards with rocks. Needless to say—no food, fires, camping, lifeguard service, etc.

MOOMMY'S MYSTERY—During a gigantic south-of-west swell a very ridable 12-foot right slide was spotted two miles south of Area Zero. Beach is private; no trespassing.

GIANT ROCK—Reef break takes a south swell. Lefts preferred to rights, which run into large rock. Location: 1 mile north of Trancas Beach. Private property; no trespassing.

Brian Donnell takes off at ZUMA BEACH. [Skipper Newton]

TRANCAS BEACH—Adjoins Zuma Beach on north and has similar waves but is in front of private property. No trespassing.

ZUMA BEACH COUNTY PARK—Waves break all along these 2 miles of beach, and rides are often extremely fast and hollow. Good fun-surf lefts and rights when surf is small. Above 4 feet peaks join to form unmakable crashing walls. Area breaks on most swells, with peaky ones best, especially when completely glassy or during light offshore winds which change already hollow waves into "suckular" tubes. Medium-to-high tides preferred. Blows out easily with south or west winds. Beach is sandy. Rips frequently present are rarely a nuisance. Room for hundreds of surfers; never crowded with boards.

Location: 19 miles above Santa Monica, 8 miles above Malibu. Los Angeles County Lifeguards on duty 9 AM to 6 PM daily. Surfing areas restricted when necessary. Emergency first-aid station is 1 mile north of main entrance to beach.

Rest rooms and food stands on beach; restaurant 2 miles north at Trancas. Parking costs 50 cents.

DRAINPIPE (WESTWARD BEACH)—Very fast hollow lefts somewhat longer than Zuma's are best on a south swell and ridable up to 8 feet. Break is in front of canyon ½ mile south of Zuma Beach; drive in on Westward Beach Road. Beach is public despite signs to contrary.

ZUMA BEACH. An icy thirty-knot offshore wind is blowing the wave crests out to sea. Gary Peterson in his wet-suit huddles beneath the spray and fights to make the wave.
[Skipper Newton]

Point Dume. Big Dume is out of sight a little to the left. At Little Dume we see: (1) Outer Reef. (2) The Point. (3) The Gully. (4) The Rock. Surf from a west swell is running 2-3 feet at The Point. (A) Highway 101.

POINT DUME—Actually there are two points here; Big Dume and Little Dume. Of the following five spots the last four are at Little Dume.

- BIG DUME—Takes a south or west swell. Ride is a right slide. Larger waves are mushy but thick and powerful; size can reach 15 feet. Swells under 6-7 feet produce peaks inside among the rocks. Quality of this small surf is sometimes good but depends on how sand distributes itself over the bottom.

- OUTER REEF—Hard-breaking peak offers steep takeoff. Surf must be 5 feet to be ridden (less at low tide, but more dangerous then because reef is shallow). Lefts which are short and hot at 6-7 feet close out completely when surf gets bigger. Rights are well-shaped, allow much turning and are rarely fast. In smaller surf rights run into rocks, but at 10-15 feet ride may continue past the Gully (about 500 yards). Takes most swells.

- THE POINT—A peaky lineup with sections and bowls. Makable at high tide. Ridable from 2 to 6-7 feet. Takes south or west swell.

- THE GULLY—Waves winding around the point peak up again here and produce both short hot lefts and long usually slow rights. Good learning spot when surf is under 4-5 feet. Larger waves break hard and offer critical takeoffs. Best at medium tide; low tide exposes rocks.

- THE ROCK—Point-like break still farther inside is ridable sometimes at 2-4 feet.

Area is seldom blown out, for west winds blow offshore. Boards lost from Outer Reef may be pounded into big rocks that line point. Remainder of beach is sandy, but most of bottom is rock-strewn. Location: 18 miles north of Santa Monica. Beach-front property in area is private, with access to beach through locked gates denied the public. Anti-trespassing law with possible $500 fine is enforced by private patrolmen and by Malibu Sheriff when called.

POINT DUME, June 1951. Buzzy Trent rides the Outer Reef as Bob Simmons watches.
[Joe Quigg]

Stuart Bailey, Outer Reef, POINT DUME. [Skipper Newton]

PARADISE COVE—Two breaks are noted.
- Just north of parking lot south swells occasionally produce 3-to-5-foot fast right walls in front of slaty rocks.
- Also there are lefts at high tide south of the pier.

Location: 17 miles north of Santa Monica. Privately owned beach resort is currently open to the swimming and fishing public but not to surfers.

LATIGO CANYON—Waves bend around point to form two basic breaks.

- THE POINT—Fairly fast takeoff over submerged rock is followed by well-shaped but slow right slide necessitating much turning or stalling to stay in hook. At medium-to-high tides you can sometimes ride to Armstrongs' Beach (300 yards). Rocks exposed at low tide have earned this spot the nickname "Ding City."
- ARMSTRONGS' BEACH—Usually a separate beach-break-type peak with fast lefts and fair rights at lower tides.

Breaks inconsistently on south and southwest swells. Ridable from 1 to 10 feet. Greatly protected from westerly winds. Strong currents when surf is large.

Location: 15 miles north of Santa Monica. Beach is private; trespassing is a misdemeanor and law is enforced by Malibu Sheriff when called by residents.

This shot of Goodwin M. "Buzzy" Trent, taken around 1950, shows LATIGO CANYON as good as it gets. [Joe Quigg]

MALIBU COLONY—Swells build outside long before breaking and seldom break hard. Rides possible in both directions with rights commoner. Too mushy for good turning or nose-riding. Breaks inconsistently on south and southwest swells. Size may reach 10 feet. Good only at lower tides; at high tide waves break too near shore. Protected from west winds by kelp. Becomes good only during offshore winds. Beach is sandy; bottom is mostly sand, but a number of large rocks are spread throughout area and are concentrated particularly at west end of beach.

Location: at foot of Malibu Canyon, 12 miles above Santa Monica. Surf is in front of fenced-off private property. Residents call sheriff to enforce anti-trespassing law.

Malibu looks like a millpond today, with a west swell producing one-foot wavelets. Malibu needs a south swell, and the 20-30 surfers here today have come because of the name, not the waves. (1) First Point, with dashed line showing flagpole lineup through Rindge Mansion (A). (2) Second Point. (3) Third Point. (4) Old Joe's. Malibu Pier at right. (B) Malibu Lagoon. (C) Malibu movie colony. (D) Highway 101.

MALIBU (SURFRIDER BEACH COUNTY PARK, MALIBU PIER)—There are four distinct surfing spots.

- FIRST POINT—When surfers say "Malibu" they mean the first point, where waves build into amazingly well-shaped right wall followed by lineup which offers maximum in turning and nose-riding for 300 yards or more—one of the best all-around surfing spots on the coast in summer. Breaks mainly on south and south-west swells; usually 2-4 feet, occasionally reaches 6-8 feet, rarely larger. A few strong west swells produce small waves here, while north swells produce absolutely nothing. Waves not always tubular but seldom mushy except at very high tides. Slightest south wind completely destroys wave quality, but normal afternoon west sea breeze comes from slightly offshore, so area seldom blows out. Small rocks begin below mean high tide line and are more numerous and sharper toward point, where spiny sea-urchins also abound.

  The classic takeoff spot is at the point in line with two of the three flagpoles in front of the Rindge Mansion. Chief cause of arguments, accidents, and general *brouhaha* is large number of people who sit farther inside and paddle into waves ahead of surfers who are already riding and thus have the right of way. However there is room for a few surfers to sit inside and take advantage of waves missed or goofed by those at the point. Even then, more than about twenty surfers make the water seem crowded. Usual summer crowd in the water: 40-100.

  From the flagpole lineup short hot lefts are sometimes possible at high tide with smaller swells.

94

- SECOND POINT—Waves bigger and hollower than at first point offer faster (frequently unmakable) but shorter rights. However freak rides from here almost to the pier have been reported. Best at medium-high incoming tide. West wind blows out surf.
- THIRD POINT—Right slide so fast as to be ridable only rarely.
- OLD JOE'S—Lefts off rocks west of Malibu Lagoon are sometimes ridable if swell is "very south"; rocks are major hazards.

Location: 11 miles north of Santa Monica, 1 mile below Malibu Canyon. Los Angeles County Lifeguard on duty 8 AM to 6 PM daily throughout year. Catering truck on beach daily in summer, weekends in winter; restaurant across highway at stop signal, two hamburger stands ½ mile below signal; supermarket 1 mile north. Gremmies notoriously mischievous; a close check on personal belongings is advisable.

SEA LION (LAS FLORES CANYON)—Right slide rarely ridable; dangerous rocks. Location: 9 miles above Santa Monica. Private beach.

BIG ROCK—Right slide rarely ridable; even more dangerous rocks. Location: 8 miles above Santa Monica. Private beach.

MALIBU. This picture, taken in 1951, may show older cars and fewer buildings than you'll see now, but the waves haven't changed. [Joe Quigg]

MALIBU takeoffs. Above: Lance Carson dropping in on the nose. Below: Harold Ige ("Iggy") fading left and turning out of the hook. [Leroy Grannis]

MALIBU turns. Above: Fred Pfahler, bottom-turn. Below: Lance Carson on the tail ready to whip a cutback, as two Malibu outriggers sail by outside. [Leroy Grannis]

NORTH BAY AREA

MALIBU crouches.
Above:
Dave Rochlen,
head-dip.
Below:
Bob Leonard,
rail-grab.
[Leroy Grannis]

MALIBU left from the First Point, by Mickey Dora. [Leroy Grannis]

MALIBU nose rides. •
Above:
Mickey Dora.

Below:
Harry "Butch" Linden.
[Leroy Grannis]

Surfing, an individual sport, in which lonely man pits his hard-won skill against the wild forces of the mighty ocean . . . MALIBU, west swell. For shots of larger Malibu waves, see page 20. [Co Rentmeester]

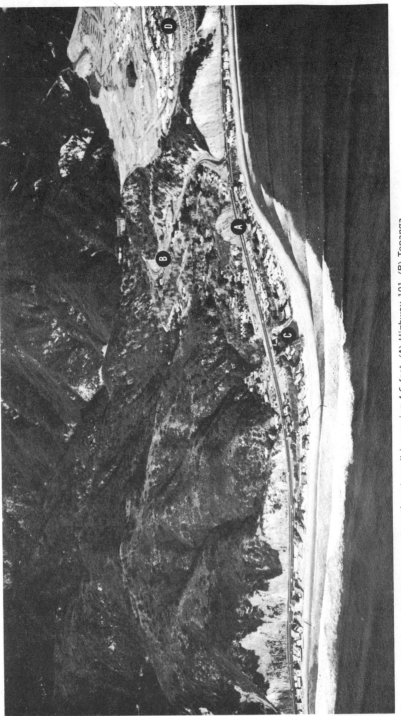

Topanga at its best. Surf from a west-southwest swell is running 4-6 feet. (A) Highway 101. (B) Topanga Canyon Boulevard. (C) Topanga River Mouth. (D) Sunset Mesa.

TOPANGA BEACH — Long sometimes makable wall at point runs into seldom makable lineup which terminates in shorebreak 300 yards to right. Breaks relatively hard over 4 feet; occasionally up to 6-8 feet. Breaks consistently in summer, but south swells assure waves unmakable for long distances. Frequently flat in winter, but area is best on freak slightly south-of-west swells, when fast tubes are occasionally makable from river mouth to traffic light (400 yards). Often good on day after local storm. Good only when glassy or during offshore winds, when waves break hardest. Blown out by south or west winds. Best at medium-to-high incoming tide; at lower tides wave develops many unmakable sections. Beach usually sandy with small sharp rocks beginning below mean high tide line; frequent dings and cut feet. Rocks decrease in size toward shorebreak, with one exception. No rips or important currents. Kelp often a nuisance.

Location: 6 miles north of Santa Monica, at foot of Topanga Canyon Boulevard. Beach (including river mouth) is privately owned. Los Angeles County ordinance makes trespassing illegal and violators are subject to possible $500 fine; uninvited surfers will find this law enforced by Malibu Sheriff who comes quickly at request of residents.

TOPANGA BEACH from Sunset Mesa. [David Stern]

Jim Fitzpatrick shoots out of a section on the nose at TOPANGA BEACH. [Co Rentmeester]

For this guidebook Professor David Stern engaged in many scholarly studies of the type shown below. He is seen here conducting an empirical investigation of the makability of south swell waves at TOPANGA BEACH. The results of this research are reported in the text on page 101. [Co Rentmeester]

POINT CAFE—Breaks only during day-after-storm surf unless swell is huge. Rarely over 4 feet. Very rocky.

SUNSET BOULEVARD—Long lines move in past point and develop into slow mushy waves on most all winter and summer swells (2-4 feet). But some larger winter swells (4-8 feet) produce good hard-breaking waves; long peak holds up and allows a fast shoot, with turning following. Small sections easily makable. Inside break poor. Usually best on lower tides, but medium tides favor larger swells. Improved by offshore winds. Blown out by south and west winds. No strong currents. Many medium-sized sharp rocks line the shore inside; at point larger submerged rocks and concrete block with projecting metal reinforcing-rods present greatest hazard. Good learning spot because waves are usually gentle.

Location: 4 miles north of Santa Monica Canyon, just below Sunset Boulevard. Area is part of Will Rogers Beach State Park. Surfing allowed all day. Los Angeles City Lifeguard on duty 10 AM to 6 PM daily in summer. Parking on highway overlooking surf. Expensive yet inferior hamburgers at restaurant 100 yards past point.

HOSHI—Right slides break near jetty north of Lighthouse at low tide. Spot's quasi-oriental name actually is formed from first few letters of two much-used English words.

LIGHTHOUSE—Swells build on variable sandbar just south of jetty. Fast takeoffs and short fast rides. Ridable from 2 to 7 feet. Breaks best on west wind swells. Spot may stay glassy a little longer than other nearby spots when sea breeze starts. Best at low tide; high creates intolerable backwash. Beach rocky, and seawall can damage boards at higher tides.

Location: ½ mile north of Santa Monica Canyon, in front of L.A. City Lifeguard headquarters. Guarded daily. Parking lot overlooks surfing area. Surfing allowed all day. Area is part of Will Rogers Beach State Park.

WILL ROGERS BEACH STATE PARK (STATE BEACH, SANTA MONICA CANYON)—Walls peak up in front of main lifeguard tower, allowing a fast beach-break shoot before shorebreak folds over. Lefts and rights sometimes well-shaped. Good fun-surf. Breaks on all swells, but much better in winter. Best on glass-offs the day after local storms, when waves up to 10 feet break on flat submerged reefs 200 or more yards from shore. Blown out easily by afternoon westerlies. Sandy beach; bottom sand and shale. Occasional rips and currents during larger swells.

Location: At foot of Santa Monica Canyon. Los Angeles City lifeguards daily 10 AM to 6 PM. Surfing prohibited 11 AM to 5 PM in summer. Rest rooms on beach. Cafes and markets across highway. Parking lot fee is 50 cents in summer, less in winter.

SANTA MONICA PIER—Sandbar sometimes builds up on south side of pier, producing right slides. Seldom reaches 6 feet. Breaks on peaky swells but best on strong winter swells. Best at lower tides. No surfing 11 AM to 5 PM in summer. Area is part of Santa Monica State Beach. Santa Monica City lifeguard headquarters is located on beach in front of surf. Guarded daily. Metered parking on streets; also private parking lots. Several cafes on pier. Location: in Santa Monica north of Pico Blvd.

SANTA MONICA BEACH—Locals call northern portion DEL MAR CLUB or BAY STREET, southern portion POP. Entire mile of beach between Santa Monica Pier and POP Pier furnishes two-way peaks which are fun up to 5 feet; larger surf usually closes out. Takes any swell, but peaky swells and day-after-storm surf best. Area favors medium-to-high tides. Santa Monica City lifeguards on duty daily. Surfing allowed all day in area at south end of beach between Lifeguard Tower #1 and POP Pier. Along rest of beach no surfing from 11 AM to 5 PM in summer and on crowded winter days. Yellow flag with black ball in center hoisted above guard towers means no surfing. Surfers must keep 100 feet from swimmers. Parking in lots costs 50 cents; metered parking on street.

Wayne Miyata in a characteristic Hawaiian-style nose stance for the surfing contest held in front of the Del Mar Club at SANTA MONICA. [Steve Pickard]

PACIFIC OCEAN PARK PIER (POP PIER)—Lefts on north side of pier become very fast and hollow at 5 to 8 feet. Rights in two different places on south side of pier depend on variable sandbars and are ridable up to 6 feet or so. Peaky surf usually best, but area can be ridden on all swells. Low tide preferred. Pier pilings a menace to boards and surfers. North side of pier is guarded by Santa Monica City lifeguards and is open to all-day surfing. South side is under jurisdiction of Los Angeles City lifeguards. Parking in lots near beach cost 50 cents.

VENICE BREAKWATER—Steep left takeoff at north end of breakwater or rights at south end are followed by a slow part of the wave and then a fast shorebreak which can be ridden left or right. Must be 4 feet to be safely ridable; seldom seen over 8. Jetty a major hazard on takeoffs, especially in smaller surf. Storm drain in shorebreak a danger sometimes. Best on winter swell.

Location: in Venice just north of Los Angeles City lifeguard headquarters, which is at foot of Windward Avenue. Area guarded daily. Beach is officially for swimming; no surfing in summer (no surf then anyhow).

HUBBYLAND—Entrance channel to the new Marina del Rey has been dredged but may still break on big west swells, much to the chagrin of its engineers. Location: in Venice at south end of Pacific Avenue, immediately north of Ballona Creek.

POP Pier. Not much surf, but a heck of an interesting-looking pier, *nicht wahr?* (1) Lefts. (2) Rights. (3) More rights. To the left of the pier is Santa Monica Beach.

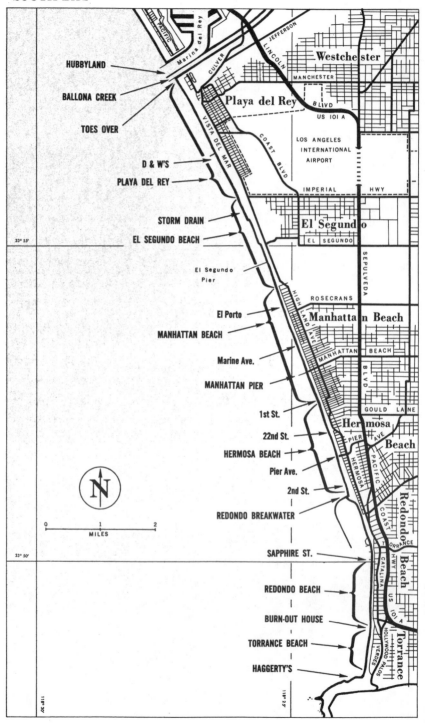

SOUTH BAY

For purposes of this book South Bay (the southern coastline of Santa Monica Bay) runs from Marina del Rey to Torrance Beach. Towns from north to south are Playa del Rey, El Segundo, Manhattan Beach, Hermosa Beach, Redondo Beach, and Torrance. Excepting the Redondo Harbor, it is physically possible to surf anywhere in the area. During unrestricted surfing hours you should be able to find uncrowded waves, even though region probably has more surfers per square mile than anywhere else in the world.

Typical beach-break peaks along most of the coast come up on any swell. Peaky wind swells, or day-after-storm surf, or days when there seem to be swells from more than one direction are best. Clear well-defined strong swells tend to line up and crash all along the beach. At many spots surf over 6 or 8 feet is not worth riding because of work involved in paddling through shorebreak, or because peaks join into unmakable walls. Surf blows out on usual west sea breeze, but area (especially southern part) may stay glassy with south winds. Surf is best in the morning before the wind comes up, or during offshore winds which hollow out waves into gremlin-devouring tubes. Beach and bottom are sandy; rip currents here and there along the beach during larger surf pose hazard only to uncertain swimmers, who shouldn't be surfing anyway.

Nearly entire area is public. There are no campgrounds. Northern portion has Los Angeles City lifeguards, southern portion Los Angeles County. All-day surfing is currently permitted at Ballona Creek, Toes Over, D & W's, El Segundo, Redondo Breakwater and Torrance Beach; of these only El Segundo and Torrance are roomy enough to accommodate a large number of surfers. In Manhattan, Hermosa, and Redondo Beaches surfing is prohibited on summer weekdays from noon to 4 PM, weekends and holidays from 11 AM to 5 PM, and occasionally in winter at guards' discretion. Watch for "no surfing" flag raised over guard towers—black ball on yellow background. Hope of establishing more all-day areas is still just a hope.

BALLONA CREEK—There are four spots.

- THE CREEK—Mouth of Ballona Creek is immediately south of Marina del Rey entrance channel. Mostly lefts, some rights; usually small and easy-breaking. Best at low to medium tides. Area somewhat protected from onshore winds but afternoon chop usually filters in and destroys glassy conditions. Cables and pipes both under and above the water are hazards.
- SOUTH JETTY—Peak in front of jetty needs big south swell. Left slide. Can reach 8 feet. Best at low tide.
- MIDDLE JETTY—Rights off the end of the jetty separating Ballona Creek from Marina del Rey need a huge winter swell.
- TOES OVER—Right slide below south jetty is named suggestively. Best at high tide, favors west swell but takes any. Quality depends on varying sand bottom.

To reach this area turn north at foot of Culver Boulevard in Playa del Rey. Los Angeles City lifeguard in tower on beach next to south jetty daily. Surfing allowed all day. Market and cafe on Culver Boulevard, ¼ mile east of surfing area.

D & W'S—Swells that peak up on sandbar south of jetty give rise to easy takeoffs but develop into extremely hot well-formed right walls. Occasionally very tubular. Little turning possible; mostly get-up-and-go. Good for nose-rides on smaller swells. Long rides on larger swells, when advisable to paddle out on north side of jetty; size reaches 10 feet. Breaks on all swells, but winter far superior. Easily blown out. Good at any tide, medium to high best. Strong currents and rips infrequent. Beach and bottom both sandy. Because of shifting sand bottom, wave characteristics fluctuate. No losing boards unnecessarily in a way that endangers another person, or out you go. Rule enforced by surfers in water who are backed by Los Angeles City lifeguard on duty in tower nearby. Surfing allowed all day. One fire pit. Location: 2 miles south of Ballona Creek at Deauville Street.

PLAYA DEL REY—Beach surf north and south of D & W'S is sometimes just as good and always less crowded. No surfing in summer.

STORM DRAIN—Fast lefts somewhat longer than usual beach rides sometimes form on north side of underwater pipeline. Quality of surf depends on bottom conditions which vary. Currents and pipes are hazards. Private property.

EL SEGUNDO BEACH—Hard-breaking beach surf between El Segundo Oil Pier and El Porto is open for all-day surfing, but access is somewhat inconvenient. Waves can reach 15 feet, at which size big peaks are seen south of the El Segundo Pier ⅓ mile or more from shore. Beach is privately owned; walk or paddle in from Manhattan Beach. Water frequently has oily scum, despite counterclaims of nearby refinery.

Gary Stever, north side of MANHATTAN PIER. [Doug Roth]

D. O. O'Connor, south side of MANHATTAN PIER. [Leroy Grannis]

Looking north at South Bay. (1) El Segundo Pier. (2) Manhattan Beach Pier. (3) Hermosa Beach. (4) Redondo Breakwater (which isn't breaking). Surf is about 3 feet all along the beach. (A) City of Manhattan Beach. (B) City of Hermosa Beach. (C) Redondo Harbor. (D) Smog.

MANHATTAN BEACH—Variety beach surf typical of that throughout South Bay breaks on any swell. EL PORTO STREET, ROSECRANS STREET, MARINE AVENUE, and FIRST STREET are popular, but fact is that one peak along the beach is likely to be as good as another, and the less known spots may be less crowded. Only place in two-mile stretch of beach requiring separate description is Manhattan Pier. Watch for "no surfing" flags over guard towers in summer. Los Angeles County lifeguards on duty in towers along beach from 8 AM to dark in summer, in stations at El Porto, Marine Street, and Manhattan Pier from 9 AM to 5 PM in winter. Gremlins on duty 24 hours a day.

MANHATTAN BEACH PIER—Peaks move in on either side of pier and produce fair to good takeoffs in both directions, depending on constantly changing bottom conditions. Good fade-turns and cutbacks possible before frequently hollow shorebreak lineup. Breaks very hard when over 4 feet. Best at 5-6 feet. Usually closes out when larger. Good nose-rides, as at all South Bay beaches. Pier can be shot. Breaks on all swells, but peaky winter surf best; strong lines tend to close out, especially those from south swells. Best at medium-to-high tide, when waves hold up longer. Blown out by south and west winds. Beach and bottom sandy. Rip under pier can be helpful in paddling out but inexperienced surfers should not attempt it. Area often crowded. Los Angeles County lifeguard in tower on pier daily. Parking lot overlooks surfing area. Cafes and markets nearby.

HERMOSA BEACH—Surfers sometimes single out LONGFELLOW STREET, 26th STREET, 22nd STREET, PIER AVENUE and SECOND STREET, and speak of mysterious "secret spots"; but plain truth is that typical beach surf is found all along this two-mile stretch of coast. Lines rise outside and peak here and there to form lefts and rights, with good turning frequently possible before hot inside lineup. Larger waves break hard. Good up to 6 feet; usually walls up when larger. Peaky winter swells best. Blown out by west and some south winds. Beach and bottom both sandy. No strong rips or currents when ridable. The famous "Zero Break" peaks which appear in front of 16th STREET about ⅓ mile from shore during gigantic winter swells were seen in 1963.

Los Angeles County lifeguards on duty daily at Pier Avenue station year round, also in towers along the beach in summer. Blackball flag over towers means no surfing. Metered parking near beach on sidestreets. Hordes of gremlins, both young and old.

Bing Copeland takes off at 22nd Street, HERMOSA BEACH. [Leroy Grannis]

Turns by Dewey Weber, 22nd Street, HERMOSA BEACH. [Leroy Grannis]

22nd Street, HERMOSA BEACH. Above: Ronald "Jeep" Shaeffer. Below: Rick Hatch.
[Leroy Grannis]

Mike Williams in El Espontaneo at 22nd Street, HERMOSA BEACH. [Leroy Grannis]

Now say "Cheese."

REDONDO BREAKWATER. [Mark Beatie]

REDONDO BREAKWATER with size. [Doug Roth]

REDONDO BREAKWATER—Large peak shifts as it moves in over submarine pipeline north of breakwater. Good turning sometimes follows steep takeoff, after which hollow wall leads to nasty shorebreak (pull out or get pounded). Ride is a left. Breaks only on large winter swells (over 6 feet) and reaches 15-20 feet. Both strong north swells and peaky day-after-storm swells break here when big enough; smaller swells from any direction produce ordinary beach surf inside. At low tide waves tend to be unmakable, while at high tide they become mushy; best at medium tide. Blown out easily by west wind, but somewhat sheltered from south wind; southeast wind blows offshore. Breakwater presents no hazard to surfers already in water, but persons walking out on it and entering surf should use extreme caution. Frequent rips and other currents when surf is big, especially at low tide next to breakwater. Beach and bottom both sandy, but at high tide boards go in to seawall. Break is located directly in front of main headquarters of Los Angeles County Lifeguard Service, at foot of Herondo Street, which forms Hermosa Beach—Redondo Beach city boundary. Guards on duty 9 AM to 8 PM year round. Surfing allowed at all times. Parking lot in front of break is generally reserved for boat-owners; if it is closed, park on Hermosa Avenue.

REDONDO BREAKWATER. The peak is unusually pronounced in this picture. [Doug Roth]

SAPPHIRE STREET—Peaks best on west swell. Lefts often better than rights. Low-medium tide preferred. Surf is usually small, but sometimes when nearby beaches are closed out at 10 feet this place will be 5 or 6 and perfect. No surfing from 11 AM to 5 PM in summer and on crowded winter weekends. Located in Redondo Beach. Park on street; walkway leads to ocean.

Jerry Wallner does a Butterfly on the nose at SAPPHIRE STREET. [John McChristy]

REDONDO BEACH—Typical beach peaks are found south of area sheltered by breakwater. AVENUE "C" and AVENUE "I" provide convenient access. Los Angeles County lifeguards at Avenue "C" year-round, and in other towers during summer. Surfing hours limited as at Hermosa; watch for blackball flag.

BURN-OUT HOUSE (BURN-DOWN, RIVIERA CLUB)—Thick peak with fast top-to-bottom wall sometimes makable when nearby beach surf lines up too much. Usually rights; lefts rare. In winter, spot may be twice as big as nearby beaches, but it is not noticeably different from them until size is 5 feet. Location: at Redondo Beach-Torrance city boundary (south end of The Esplanade).

TORRANCE BEACH—Peaks rise up outside producing good lefts and rights all along the beach. Most popular (crowded) spot is at foot of ramp. Area takes north and west swells; peaky wind swells in summer can be ridden, with best place being south of ramp. West wind produces chop, but south wind blows from land. Los Angeles County lifeguards on duty here daily year round. Area from 100 yards below guard station southward for half a mile is reserved for all-day surfing throughout the year. Parking above ramp in lot costs 50 cents in summer.

Mike O'Neil, TORRANCE BEACH. [John McChristy]

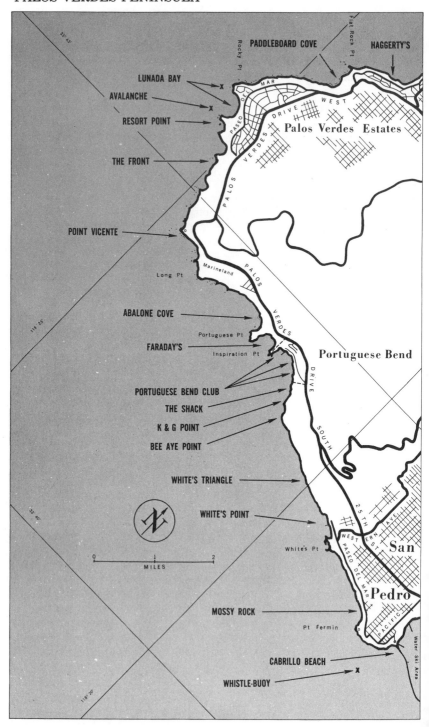

PALOS VERDES PENINSULA

Steep cliffs and rocky coastline with reef breaks predominate. There is very little beach surf. Much of the coast is unsurfable. Even at the surfable spots wipeouts are often expensive in terms of dings and broken boards. Main road through area is Palos Verdes Drive; here and there Paseo del Mar branches off toward the ocean. Towns are Palos Verdes Estates, Portuguese Bend, and San Pedro. World-famous Marineland Oceanarium is located just west of Portuguese Bend. No camp grounds.

Johnny Goodwin, HAGGERTY'S. [Leroy Grannis]

PALOS VERDES PENINSULA

Haggerty's. (1) Main break. Note pilings. Twenty-five surfers are vying for six-foot waves. (2) Lower Haggerty's. (3) Ratchet. Upper Haggerty's lies outside the picture to the right. Torrance Beach and the rest of South Bay are outside the picture to the left. (A) Palos Verdes Drive. (B) Paseo del Mar. (C) Private road past swimming club to bottom of cliff.

HAGGERTY'S. Swimming clubhouse in foreground. [John Clemens]

HAGGERTY'S (MALAGA COVE)—Lines wind around point and become ridable in several places.

- HAGGERTY'S main break is near pilings, where large peak which builds far outside produces a good takeoff followed by exclusively left slide of up to 200 yards. North swell makes wave well-shaped and fairly fast; west swell produces peakier lineup, so that ride consists of shooting through sections followed by turning and/or stalling to stay near hook; south swell is useless. Wave has quality at 5-6 feet and can be ridden at 10-12. At high tide only the biggest swells break; at low tide wave sucks out over shallow and dangerous rocks; medium tide is best. South winds blow offshore here and cliff protects area somewhat from southwest winds, but west and north winds blow out the surf. Lost boards are carried into hungry rocks which emit efficient board-digesting enzymes; usual mealtime is high tide. More than 7-8 surfers make area feel crowded.

- UPPER HAGGERTY'S—Farther out on the point are bigger, faster, hollower more unmakable lefts. The rocks are bigger too. Paddle out one-third mile from main break. Area is rarely surfed.

- LOWER HAGGERTY'S—A small peak 300 yards inside the main break. Rights preferred to lefts. Best at low tide.

- RATCHET, SCRATCHIT, or something like that—Another little left still farther inside; the first reef south of Torrance Beach.

Location: One-half mile west of Palos Verdes Estates shopping center on Paseo del Mar. Currently private club in front of Lower Haggerty's allows surfers to walk (but not drive) down their road to the beach. Dirt trail down cliff directly in front of main break is critical under any circumstances and impossible after heavy rains.

Rick Irons, LOWER HAGGERTY'S. Torrance Beach in background. [Jim Cardillo]

Paddleboard Cove. (1) The Channel. Note how the wave backs off inside. (2) Little Queens. (3) Ski Jump (not breaking). (4) The Indicator, breaking about ten feet. (A) Palos Verdes Drive. (B) Paseo del Mar. (C) Trail down cliff.

Riding high at "The Channel," PADDLEBOARD COVE. [Jim Cardillo]

PADDLEBOARD COVE. A ten-foot wave breaking at the Channel is very ridable. The Indicator (far left) seems to be between sets. [David Stern]

PADDLEBOARD COVE, BLUFF COVE, PALOS VERDES COVE or just plain **THE COVE**—There are several ridable reefs.

- THE CHANNEL—Main break near center of bay starts to work at 3 feet; lefts usually close out at 5-8 feet, rights at 8-10. Waves are thick and ride is frequently but not always slow. In smaller surf wave backs off inside, leaving boards lost in wipeouts floating unharmed in calm water. In larger surf loose boards nearly always go in to the rocks. Features combine to make area excellent learning spot when swell is running 3-6 feet.

- LITTLE QUEEN'S (NORTH REEF)—On north side of bay is fast tubular fun-surf from 2 to 4 feet; larger waves close out. Rights better than lefts. Medium-to-high tide preferred.

- THE INDICATOR (STEEPCLIFF)—Break off south point of bay reaches 15-20 feet. Very fast and steep takeoff is followed by fast left slide. Lost boards are battered against rocks inside. High tide essential unless surf is huge.

- SKI JUMP—Reef in front of Flatrock Point on north side of cove must be at least 10 feet to break and can reach 15-20 feet. Good takeoff is followed by right slide which can be long but is not very fast.

Area takes winter swells, though big summer swells produce some good surf. Entire area is blown out by west winds, but south and east winds blow offshore. In big surf watch for currents near edges of bay. Location: 1 mile west of Palos Verdes Estates shopping center on Paseo del Mar. Broad half-mile trail descends to cove from north. Parking at top of trail.

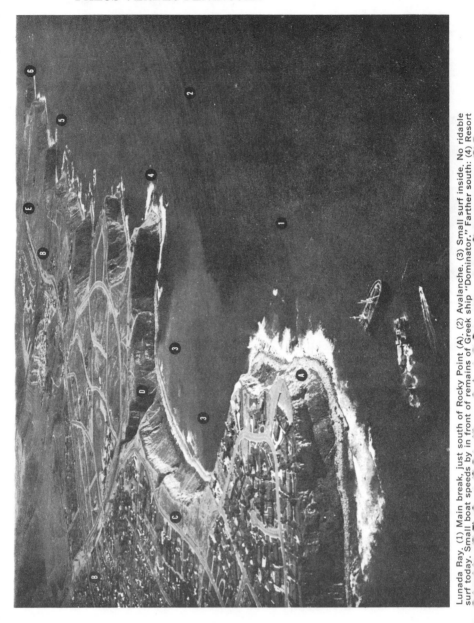

Lunada Bay. (1) Main break, just south of Rocky Point (A). (2) Avalanche. (3) Small surf inside. No ridable surf today. Small boat speeds by in front of remains of Greek ship "Dominator." Farther south: (4) Resort

LUNADA BAY—There are three spots.

- ROCKY POINT—Swells move in on north side of bay and build deceptively on the uneven rocky bottom into steep, fast, hard-breaking, angry, ugly, nasty, mean right walls. Size can exceed 20 feet, which makes spot a promising candidate for Southern California's biggest surf award. Surf under 8 feet breaks dangerously close to rocks. Takes north and west swells. Higher tides better and safer. Bottom, which looks like the face of the moon, creates annoying boils and turbulence. Rocks both on shore and submerged present grave hazards to surfers. The battered hulk of the Greek ship "Dominator," grounded nearby and now broken in half, is an ever-present reminder of the probable fate of boards lost in wipeouts. Very strong currents near shore and in center of bay can tire all but the best swimmers. Summing up the place one of the regulars says, "A critical takeoff, a critical ride—you're in jeopardy just being there."

- AVALANCHE—Lefts break on exposed reefs in front of Resort Point on south side of bay. They can arise on any swell and reach 12 feet. Surf at 6-8 feet consists of a fast peak takeoff which bowls around and can pick you off before you reach the flat shoulder. Area is even rockier than north side of bay.

- INSIDE—Smaller ridable breaks are found inside the cove itself; rocks are still dangerous.

Location: Two miles below Paddleboard Cove, three miles above Marineland. Park on south side of gully and descend trail (hard to find) near its mouth. Nearest food, water, etc. a few blocks north and inland on Palos Verdes Drive.

RESORT POINT—Rights in the cove just south of Lunada Bay section dangerously in front of a rock and are rarely worth riding.

THE FRONT—Short lefts best on a south swell. Closes out at 6 feet. Wave backs off leaving lost boards in calm water. Location: off Palos Verdes Drive ⅔ mile south of Lunada Bay. No parking on private beach property.

POINT VICENTE—Rights reported ridable at 6-7 feet. Very rocky. Located just west of Marineland.

Surf's up at LUNADA BAY. [David Stern]

Greg Noll, LUNADA BAY. [Alan Rich]

Sailboat breezes by with no concern for the swell which a few hundred yards inside is producing rides like this—at LUNADA BAY. [Jim Cardillo]

Greg Noll, LUNADA BAY. [Jim Noll]

". . . angry, nasty, mean right walls" at LUNADA BAY. Greg Noll riding. Surfer at right tried to paddle over the wave, saw it break, turned around and is now making an heroic attempt to prone out. Lots of luck!
[Jim Cardillo]

(1-2) Abalone Cove: (1) Beach surf. (2) Point surf. (3) Faraday's. (4-6) Portuguese Bend Club: (4) Pier Point. (5) Beach. (6) Seawall. (7) The Shack. (8) K & G Point. (9) Bee Aye Point. (A) Portuguese Point. (B) Inspiration Point. (C) Palos Verdes Drive. Marineland is to left, outside the picture.

ABALONE COVE—Three ridable spots are noted.

- Lefts appear off Portuguese Point at east side of cove on west swell. Best over 5 feet, may reach 10-12. Faster at low tide.
- Beach surf usually walls up and crashes but becomes ridable during peaky swells.
- Large peak is reported to break just west of center of cove during huge west swells.

Location: 1 mile east of Marineland. Area is private and fenced off but can be rented for beach parties.

FARADAY'S (M & I'S)—Lefts along east side of tiny bay separating Abalone Cove from Portuguese Bend Club. Rocks a nuisance under 3 feet. Closes out over 6.

PORTUGUESE BEND CLUB—Surf is ridable in three areas.

- PIER POINT (THE PIER, INSPIRATION POINT)—Comes up on larger winter swells (6-15 feet). Takeoff is steep but ride is slow. If surf is big enough you can ride past the pier. Large rock in break can be a hazard, depending on swell size. Best at medium-to-high tide.
- THE BEACH—Ordinary beach-break under 4 feet, but larger waves break on outside reefs which run from the Seawall to Pier Point. Good up to 8 feet. Favors south swell and higher tides.
- THE SEAWALL—Reef just west of seawall produces rides in either direction, with well-formed right lineup in winter and superior lefts in summer. Peaky swells produce break closer to seawall itself.

Location: 3 miles east of Marineland. The area is a private community with a gatekeeper always on duty. Access is next to impossible for anyone but residents and their guests.

THE SHACK—Take off fading left toward rock, then turn into right slide as wave re-forms. Winter swells best. Ridable from 3 to 6 feet. High tide produces backwash and makes waves mushy; low tide exposes rocks: best at medium tide. Location: just inside K & G Point.

K & G POINT—A steep fast left on a big summer swell (6-10 feet). Rocks inside a menace. Located ½ mile east of Portuguese Bend Club gate at foot of private dirt road.

BEE AYE POINT—Another left on a big south swell (8-15 feet). Waves section in front of a rock at 10-plus, but at 8 feet you can sometimes squeeze by. Location: ⅓ mile east of K & G Point.

WHITE'S TRIANGLE—Peak ¾ mile west of White's Point comes up on a west swell. Virtually inaccessible.

WHITE'S POINT (ROYAL PALMS)—There are two spots, neither of which is the point labeled White's Point on most maps.

- Lefts break just west of the jetty on smaller swells.
- Rights break off the point 300 yards west when surf reaches 6-12 feet. Larger surf may close out the cove.

Rocks and treacherous water a hazard when paddling out. Area good during storms, when usual winds blow offshore. Medium-high tide best; low tide makes waves suck out over rocks. Location: at foot of Western Avenue. Park along Paseo del Mar above and walk down road (usually chained off) to surfing area. No facilities available to public on beach. Los Angeles City lifeguard in tower 10 AM to 6 PM daily in summer, weekends in winter.

MOSSY ROCK—Surf peaks up over reefs in cove ⅓ mile west of Point Fermin Lighthouse. Lefts off east side of cove, rights off west side, peaks in middle. Short rides. Takes south or west swell. Best size is 4 feet; waves section at 5-6. Beach and bottom rocky. Paths lead down cliff.

THE WHISTLE-BUOY—East of Point Fermin surf appears over reef marked by groaning whistle-buoy. Takes a big north swell. Right slide. Must be 6 feet to break, reaches 10-12.

CABRILLO BEACH STATE PARK—In winter fast takeoff runs into makable wall followed by slower lineup. Rides sometimes quite long. In summer deceptively shifting but not hard-breaking peak at west end of beach is best spot. Medium-to-high tides preferred. Area blown out easily in winter but is somewhat protected in summer by Palos Verdes Peninsula. New jetty built out from breakwater is trapping sand and changing the surf somewhat.

Location: in San Pedro just east of Point Fermin at foot of Stephen M. White Drive. Dressing rooms, with hot showers. Fire pits on beach; snack bars nearby. Los Angeles City lifeguard on duty 8 AM to 1 PM in summer, 10 AM to 6 PM in winter, on beach or in headquarters building behind guard tower. Surfing all day in marked areas except when beach is very crowded. Freeboarding (being pulled by boat) possible in water-ski area behind breakwater (see photo, page 227).

(1) Cabrillo Beach, with new jetty at extreme right. (2) The Whistle-Buoy. (3) Water-ski area of Los Angeles Harbor. (A) City of San Pedro.

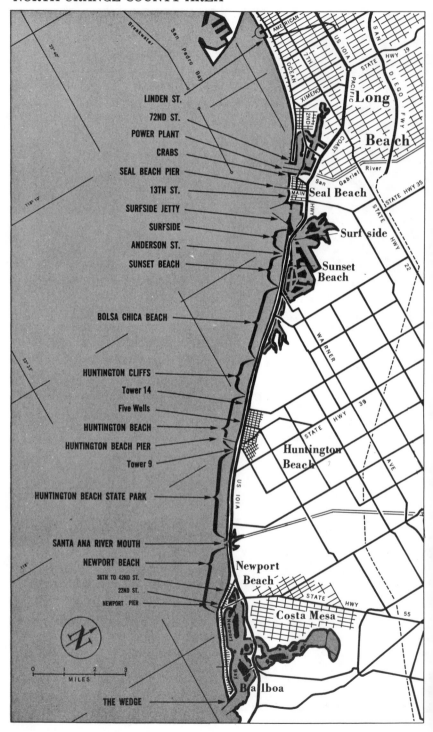

NORTH ORANGE COUNTY AREA

Long Beach Harbor on the north and Balboa Harbor on the south form the limits to this area. Most of it is sandy beach, with typical beach surf breaking all along; a number of piers and jetties add spice and variety. Unfortunately some of the coastline in greatest demand by surfers is not available for all-day surfing. On the other hand there are stretches of beach with fair to good surf that no one uses much even when surfing is permitted. Starting at the north, the towns in this area are: Long Beach, Naples, Seal Beach, Surfside, Sunset Beach, Huntington Beach, Newport Beach, and Balboa. Across Balboa Bay from Newport Beach is Costa Mesa. There are no campgrounds; closest ones are Doheny Beach State Park and San Clemente Beach State Park to south.

LINDEN STREET (RAINBOW PIER)—Waves peak up over sandbar near jetty. Rights better than lefts, which head into jetty. Spot is feeble reminder of the famous Flood Control surf which used to break nearby and was destroyed by building of Long Beach Breakwater. Now it breaks only on very strong south swell, which must sneak in between two breakwaters; size is rarely over 4 feet.

Location: Long Beach. Beach is public. Surfing allowed all day. Long Beach City lifeguard on duty 9 AM to 8 PM in summer, 9 AM to 5 PM in winter.

72ND STREET—Point-like break north of jetty offers easy takeoff followed by long hollow lefts. "West" swell must be south enough to pass around Long Beach Breakwater; but true south swell is poor. Place must be 3 feet to break and is hardly ever bigger, with 6 feet absolute maximum. Rest of beach west to 62nd Street offers generally tiny and poor beach surf but is reserved for surfing.

Located in Naples; drive east from Long Beach on Ocean Boulevard. Long Beach City lifeguards on duty 9 AM to 8 PM in summer, 9 AM to 5 PM in winter.

Mike Haley on an inside wave at SEAL BEACH POWER PLANT. [Robert von Sternberg]

SEAL BEACH POWER PLANT (RAY BAY)—Line peaks up over consistently located sandbar between two jetties enclosing San Gabriel River Mouth, directly in front of power plant. Easy takeoff is followed by well-shaped lineup. Rights longer than lefts. Hard initial break quickly loses power, as water deepens inside, so that pushing through is easy. Breaks only on south swell; best at medium-to-high tide; can reach 8 feet. Protected from wind by jetties; seldom blown out. No hard rips or strong currents, but bothersome backwash inside because of jetties. Power plant keeps water temperature near 90 degrees, attracting many stingrays (painful) and sand sharks (harmless). Cooler water outside. Parking in lot at foot of First Street costs 50 cents. Lunchwagon there in summer. Surfing all day. Seal Beach City lifeguard on duty nearby in summer. Like gremmyville.

CRABS—Fairly fast right slide on south side of jetty breaks on south swell, can reach 6 feet. Low tide best. Blows out rather easily. Fewer stingrays than at Power Plant, which is on other side of jetty. No surfing 10 AM to 6 PM May 1 to October 1. Seal Beach City lifeguard on duty in summer.

Rich Chew picks a difficult position on the nose at SEAL BEACH PIER. [Robert von Sternberg]

SEAL BEACH PIER—Swell bounces off cement wall on north side of pier and upon being reflected causes peak to move across succeeding wave; takeoff in this peak is followed by well-shaped frequently hollow left lineup. Rides usually short. Good up to 6 or 7 feet. Breaks on winter swells, but only north swell produces these shifting peaks. West swell waves are more like ordinary beach surf, though often better than that nearby. On southwest swell waves break on both sides of the pier; but spot is poor on true south swell. Waves have best shape at medium tide. Area easily blown out; improved greatly by offshore winds. Beach and bottom sandy. Main lifeguard station for City of Seal Beach is located at pier; guards on duty year round 9 AM to 6 PM. Dressing rooms. Fire pits. Many snack bars and markets nearby. As this book goes to press, word has been received that all of Seal Beach south of Second Street has been closed to surfing for an indefinite period because of the acts of the unruly and the careless. Negotiations to have the beach reopened are underway between local surfers and the City Council; the plan most likely to be adopted is one in which surfboards would be licensed by the city and the opening and closing of beaches would be subject to the immediate discretion of the Seal Beach city lifeguard service.

King Neptune claws at Eddie "Barrymore" Howard. THIRTEENTH STREET, Seal Beach.
[Robert von Sternberg]

13TH STREET—Deceptive moving peak breaks hard upon hitting sandbars and offers critical takeoff followed by hollow wall ending in treacherous shorebreak. Lefts usually better than rights. Must be 4 feet to break, occasionally reaches 12. Takes winter swell but breaks seldom. Low tide preferred. Beach public. Lifeguard tower not manned in winter. Market at 14th Street. Location: Seal Beach. Area is now closed to surfing (see previous page).

SURFSIDE JETTY—Wide powerful thick peaks break south of jetty and offer long well-shaped right lineup ending in bone-jarring shorebreak. Low tide best; wave tends to mush out at higher tides. Must be 6 feet to break, and reaches 20—big enough to break past end of jetty, over ⅔ mile from shore. Takes winter swell. Jetty and seawall on beach destroy boards. Character of peak depends on shifting sand bottom. Direct access is through private colony of homes which has the dubious distinction of being declared a disaster area whenever the surf comes up. Nearest public entry is from Anderson Street, about a mile south.

Robert "Smitty" von Sternberg on a small SURFSIDE JETTY wave.

Pete Kobsev, WATER TOWER. [Robert von Sternberg]

SURFSIDE—Similar to Sunset Beach.

SUNSET BEACH —Fast beach peaks are best at medium-to-high tide; low tide produces unridable walls. Takes any swell, with south often good. Ridable to 6 feet; larger surf hard to push through. Blown out by normal sea breeze in afternoon. Sand beach and bottom. ANDERSON STREET (WATER TOWER), at north end of town, next to Surfside, is most popular area. Look up and down beach to find uncrowded waves, if any. Beach public. Huntington Beach City lifeguards patrol area by jeep and in summer from towers. No surfing June 1 to October 1 from 11 AM to 5 PM. Intense gremlin problem threatens surfing future here. Cafes on nearby Highway 101.

BOLSA CHICA BEACH STATE PARK (TIN CAN BEACH)—Somewhat mushy but quite serviceable beach peaks along three miles of coast. Blows out on west wind. No surfing at all in summer except along south quarter-mile of beach, where it is allowed all day. Huntington Beach City lifeguards on duty in summer. Often uncrowded. Location: Between Huntington Beach and Sunset Beach.

Huntington Cliffs. Plenty of surf, size about 4 feet. In an aerial photograph these waves appear as beautiful peaks. Only from below is their mushy character revealed.

HUNTINGTON CLIFFS—Long lines usually build into very fat mushy walls with poor shape. Surf over 6 feet breaks harder, but rides are seldom worth the effort of pushing through. Lots of room to take off and lots of waves rolling in make this mile-long stretch of beach an excellent learning spot; beginners can use time spent in long soupy swims for lost boards to contemplate their mistakes. Waves break on all swells, getting biggest and sometimes well-shaped in winter. Any tide is all right, but higher tide makes waves hold up longer. Blown out easily by south winds; offshore winds improve waves immeasurably, occasionally permitting good rides. Sand-gravel bottom; sand beach (but watch for broken glass).

Location: 2 miles north of Huntington Pier. Surfing allowed all day by City of Huntington Beach, whose lifeguards are on duty in area daily in summer and patrol by jeep the rest of the year. Parking along highway adjoining beach. Markets, cafes, etc. in city of Huntington Beach.

HUNTINGTON BEACH—Four miles of city-owned beach center around the Huntington Beach Pier. Surfers single out:

• TOWER 14—Surf near lifeguard tower 1½ miles north of pier.
• FIVE WELLS—Surf in front of five oil wells between Highway 101 and the ocean.
• TOWER 9—Located ½ mile south of pier.

The surf in the area resembles that near Huntington Pier itself, which is described on the next page. Surfing is allowed all day the year round in the Tower 14-Five Wells area; south of the pier it is prohibited June 1 to September 15 between 11 AM and 5 PM.

An unknown surfer hangs at the top of a long wall about to crash over, just north of the HUNTINGTON BEACH PIER. [Mike Gaughan]

Huntington Beach Pier. The "surf of champions" is about 3-4 feet high in the picture. Eight or ten surfers are waiting on the south side for something a little larger. Highway 101 along the shore is crowded with weekend traffic.

HUNTINGTON BEACH PIER—On both sides of the pier waves may build on sandbars into well-shaped peaks followed by good lineups in either direction. Best known are summer lefts on south side, but in winter rights on north side are frequently preferable. Most often ridden at 3 to 6 feet; occasionally ridable at 8-plus. High tide makes the characteristically thick waves mushy, while low tide tends to destroy their shape; waves break hard and hold shape best at medium tide. Blown out by west or south wind. Bottom is sandy, and shifting sandbars can alter the quality of the surf from year to year and day to day. Easiest place to paddle out is on either side of pier right next to pilings, for pier forms deeper channel which keeps smaller waves from breaking. The inexperienced surfer should not attempt even this maneuver—let alone shooting the pier—as the mussel-covered pilings of the pier can destroy lost boards and severly injure people.

Often overpopulated near pier, but beach surf on either side is sometimes just as good and never as crowded. Metered parking available near pier. Dressing rooms, 10¢. Fire pits. Many nearby snackbars, cafes. City lifeguard headquarters in on beach south of pier. Guards there daily. No surfing between 11 AM and 5 PM from June 1 to September 15.

Ron Sizemore performs at the West Coast Surfing Championships held annually at HUNTING-TON BEACH PIER. [Leroy Grannis]

HUNTINGTON BEACH STATE PARK—Frequently good beach surf—tubes, peaks, walls; nose-rides, turns, and all that. Surfing is usually allowed all day at south end of beach because of interesting administrative procedure: starting at north end of park, only enough beach is opened to general (swimming) public to accomodate crowd. Park officials do not object to surfers who walk in from Highway 101 at Santa Ana River Mouth so long as they stay away from swimmers. No lifeguard service at south end of beach when surfing is allowed. Surfing anywhere along beach in winter.

141

(1) Santa Ana River Mouth. Surfers are sitting in south channel for some reason. Note submerged fifth jetty (A) just north of the others. (2) Huntington Beach State Park. City of Newport Beach is at right.

SANTA ANA RIVER MOUTH—There are two surfing areas.

- For learners, the flat easy-breaking surf between the jetties offers straight-off rides.
- Out in front of the four jetties waves build into beach-break-type peaks with fast takeoff in either direction followed by extremely fast lineup. Breaks on all swells, and usually a little bigger than nearby beach surf. Lefts fast with south swell; also good quality on peaky winter swells. With light offshore winds, waves become tubular and even faster. South swells over 6 feet line up too much, so that peaks join into unridable walls. Blown out easily by west wind. Beach and bottom are sandy, but lost boards can be damaged by jetties. Very strong rips and currents in larger surf. Submerged fifth jetty to north a dangerous hazard to the uninformed.

Location: North of Newport Beach. Newport Beach City lifeguard is on duty just south of southernmost jetty during summer months. Area is open all day to surfing, but surfers must stay north of southernmost jetty in summer. Parking on small side-streets near area.

42ND STREET TO SANTA ANA RIVER—Beach between Santa Ana River Mouth and 42nd Street in Newport Beach offers fair peaks in winter (when surfing is permitted all day), walls up and closes out on south swells (in summer—when surfing is prohibited anyway).

36TH STREET TO 42ND STREET—This beach-break is active both winter and summer, the latter producing eminently better waves. Usual peaks in this area give rise to good short lefts and rights. But on strong south swells peaks join in large wall and only makable ride is the left at the north end of the wall—very fast and occasionally quite long. Best shape usually comes with higher tides. Area is blown out easily by west winds. Beach and bottom sandy. Rips infrequent; side-currents at times very strong. Portions of beach where surfing is allowed are changed from week to week and marked by flags. No surfing before 7:30 AM or between noon and 6 PM, June through September. Parking only on side-streets in residential area. As on all Newport and Corona del Mar beaches, beware of Police, both in uniform and disguised as tourists, whose main mission seems to be to rid the city of such heinous criminals as beach beer-drinkers, unleashed dogs, and surfers who change clothes in their cars.

22ND STREET TO 36TH STREET—Good on west swell, nothing on south. No surfing in summer.

Mike Lutes, 38th STREET, Newport Beach. Ilima Kalama (left) watches. [Tom Jewell]

Danny Lenahan, 38th STREET, Newport Beach. [Robert von Sternberg]

Mike Lutes, 38th STREET, Newport Beach. [Tom Jewell]

Kent Haworth, 38th STREET, Newport Beach. [Tom Jewell]

Newport Beach. (1) Twenty-second Street. About 20 surfers out for 3-foot waves. (2) Newport Pier. Behind is Newport Bay. (A) Newport Boulevard. (B) Balboa Boulevard. (C) Highway 101.

22ND STREET—Beach break consists of peaks offering fast rides of varying lengths in both directions. In winter best surf is a couple hundred yards north of Newport Pier; lefts are longer and steeper. Surf usually 2 to 5 feet. Best at higher tides; especially good during offshore winds, when waves become very hollow. Blown out easily by west wind. Beach and bottom sandy. No surfing in summer. Lifeguards on duty in roving jeep. Parking lot immediately adjoining pier has 25¢ meters which are closely scrutinized by Police. Several markets and cafes in immediate area.

NEWPORT PIER—Beach from pier to 20th Street offers small slow waves on south swell, but area is open to surfing in summer from 6 AM to 12 noon and again from 6 PM to sunset. Surfers must stay 20 feet from pier.

Kent Haworth, 22nd STREET, Newport Beach. [Tom Jewell]

Al Doesburg, THE WEDGE. In the foreground is...sand. [Tom Jewell]

Nancy Gardner bodysurfing at the Wedge. [Bud Browne]

See the pretty sailboats leaving Newport Bay. With a west swell the Wedge (1) is breaking about two inches high. Ditto Corona del Mar Jetty (2). But wait till summer! City across the channel is Corona del Mar.

THE WEDGE—Swells move along jetty forming large peak (wall) permitting good body-surfing. First wave of a set creates backwash that bounces from jetty across second wave, making it more peakish— consequently more shape and better ride. Second wave does same to third, etc. Very thick waves tube top-to-bottom, throwing water far out— generally too steep for board-surfing. Frequently 4-7 feet, but occasionally exceeds 15. Only extreme south swells produce good surf here: completely walled-out on other swells. Blown out by west wind. Soupy water, strong backwash, and huge rip on north side of peak as well as other strong currents make area dangerous for any but experienced watermen. Best-known hazard is that large waves break tremendously hard in shallow water, facilitating existence-negation.

Located in Balboa at end of peninsula. Body-surfing is permitted all day. Area supervised from a jeep by Newport Beach lifeguard; nearest tower is at "L" Street.

Leon Montapert roars down the mountain with fins and bellyboard at THE WEDGE. [Tom Jewell]

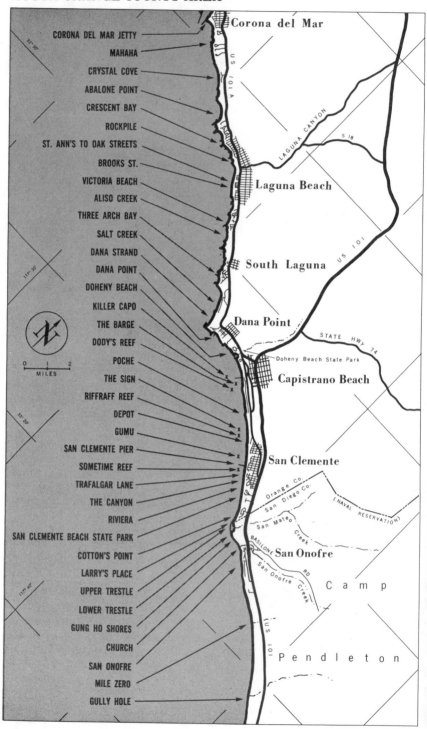

CORONA DEL MAR JETTY
MAHAHA
CRYSTAL COVE
ABALONE POINT
CRESCENT BAY
ROCKPILE
ST. ANN'S TO OAK STREETS
BROOKS ST.
VICTORIA BEACH
ALISO CREEK
THREE ARCH BAY
SALT CREEK
DANA STRAND
DANA POINT
DOHENY BEACH
KILLER CAPO
THE BARGE
DODY'S REEF
POCHE
THE SIGN
RIFFRAFF REEF
DEPOT
GUMU
SAN CLEMENTE PIER
SOMETIME REEF
TRAFALGAR LANE
THE CANYON
RIVIERA
SAN CLEMENTE BEACH STATE PARK
COTTON'S POINT
LARRY'S PLACE
UPPER TRESTLE
LOWER TRESTLE
GUNG HO SHORES
CHURCH
SAN ONOFRE
MILE ZERO
GULLY HOLE

Corona del Mar

Laguna Beach

South Laguna

Dana Point

Doheny Beach State Park

Capistrano Beach

San Clemente

San Onofre

Camp

Pendleton

0 1 2
MILES

SOUTH ORANGE COUNTY AREA

Between Balboa Bay and Dana Point most of the coast is rocky, with deep water near shore and not much ridable surf. From Dana Point south to San Onofre a shallow shelf extends seaward and in places waves break on reefs several hundred yards out. Towns from north to south are: Corona del Mar, Laguna Beach, South Laguna, Dana Point, Capistrano Beach, San Clemente, and San Onofre. Campgrounds are at Doheny and San Clemente Beach State Parks.

CORONA DEL MAR JETTY—Swell builds up on north side of jetty into a right wall that holds up long enough for short but very fast nose-rides. Wave is tubular and breaks hard. Breaks only on south swells and gets up to 8 feet. On larger swells rides may be picked up at end of jetty. Right slide is necessary to avoid crashing into jetty. Ride continues until wave walls up inside, where tremendous wipeouts can be expected. Low tide makes waves unridable (they wall up more). Higher tide and prevailing west wind (which blows offshore here) hold up waves longer.

Turn off Highway 101 at Marguerite Avenue in Corona del Mar. Parking lot adjoins beach: fee is 50¢ weekdays, $1.00 weekends and holidays. In summer no surfing noon to 6 PM weekdays, 10 AM to 6 PM weekends and holidays. Surfing all day in winter. Surfing area posted. Newport Beach City lifeguards on duty 10 AM to 8 PM. Fire pits, food stand, restrooms. Beach closes at 10 PM.

MAHAHA (CAMEO SHORES COVE)—Peaks build on submerged reefs and allow both rights and lefts. Waves deceptive due to irregular bottom. Best from 3 to 5 feet; usually closes out when larger. Breaks on all swells, with peaky winter swells preferred. Medium tide gives peaks good shape. Blows out easily. Beach is sandy, but bottom is strewn with large rocks which cause frequent dings, missing skegs and "surprise" wipeouts. Kelp also bothersome. No major currents when ridable.

Location: Cameo Shores Drive, 1 mile south of Corona del Mar. Dirt trail leads south to beach. Infrequency of good waves makes effort of walking and violation of private property rights seldom worthwhile.

SCOTCHMAN'S COVE—Mainly body-surfing. In summer public may pay to park on privately owned land and use trail down cliff to beach. Closed in winter (not much surf then anyhow).

Looking north from Laguna Beach. (1) Brooks Street. (2) Oak Street. (3) Anita Street. (4) Thalia Street. (5) Saint Ann's Street. (6) Rockpile. (7) Crescent Bay. (8) Abalone Point. (9) Crystal Cove. (10) Scotchman's Cove, Mahaha, and Corona del Mar. (11) Newport Pier. (A) Highway 101.

CRYSTAL COVE—Mainly body-surfing; private property.

ABALONE POINT—Lefts off the point occasionally. Location: At El Morro Trailer Park 2 miles north of Laguna Beach, where Highway 101 dips down to sea level. Private property.

CRESCENT BAY—Body-surfing only. Private.

ROCKPILE—There are three places to ride.

- BIRD ROCK—Lefts possible on a strong south swell, but break is inconsistent. Best at 3 to 6 feet; larger surf closes out.
- ROCKPILE—Reef break, lefts and rights, takes most swells and is fairly consistent. Ridable up to 6 feet, then walls up.
- THE POINT—Rights unridable under 3 feet because of rocks; occasionally reaches 8 feet. Breaks on most larger swells.

Location: in front of Laguna Beach Municipal Art Gallery. No surfing 11 AM to 5 PM, June through September. Area patrolled by Laguna Beach City lifeguard in summer.

152

Chris Kaspir, CRESCENT BAY. [Robin Commagere]

ST ANN'S, THALIA, ANITA, OAK STREETS—Waves build over reefs into peaky walls which frequently offer good beach-break-type rights and lefts. Best spot usually just north of Oak Street, but not always. Best surf not always where most people are. Waves not tubular but usually fast. Breaks on all swells, but south swells wall up all the way from Brooks Street and are nearly unridable. Good only on westerly swells from 3 to 6 feet at medium tide. Blows out on west wind, but usually stays glassy longer than nearby areas. Beach sandy. Currents seldom if ever strong and rips infrequent. Only hazards are a few submerged rocks in general area, but these are not a major danger. Laguna Beach City lifeguard on duty in summer. From June 1 to September 30, surfing hours are limited to before 11 AM and after 5 PM. Parking on side-streets in front of private homes. Food a couple blocks away. Location: Laguna Beach.

BROOKS STREET—Wave builds on submerged reefs into unpredictable left wall. Very fast takeoff precedes an even faster and usually un-makable lineup which walls up and comes over extremely hard. Wipe-outs especially spectacular in shorebreak. Size reaches 10 feet. Breaks off reefs only on summer swell; winter swell produces average beach surf fifty yards south. Low tide destroys shape inside, while high tide keeps waves from building on reefs; best at medium tide. Waves often bumpy, due to backwash and boils. Blown out by predominant westerly winds, but patchy kelp outside helps preserve glassy conditions some-what. Few rips and strong currents unless surf is large. Beach mostly sandy, but at higher tides lost boards smash into rocks just above shore. Sunken reefs and rocks, often detectable by aforementioned boils on water surface, comprise main danger to surfers during wipeouts. Excellent body-surfing here, but same warnings apply even more strongly.

Location: in Laguna Beach, one block south of Oak Street. No surfing from 11 AM to 5 PM in summer. City lifeguards on duty a few blocks north in summer.

A typically bumpy BROOKS STREET wave. [Bruce Brown]

VICTORIA COVE, ALISO CREEK, CAMEL POINT, AND WEST STREET—These four spots are public and good mainly for body-surfing on medium to big swells. The last three are within ½ mile of each other just south of Laguna Beach. Guarded in summer by San Clemente City lifeguards.

SEAFAIR LODGE—Small peaks on wind swells and south swells. Location: 1 mile above South Laguna.

THREE ARCH BAY—Surf in tiny cove just north of Mussel Cove is rarely good but sometimes ridden. Location: ⅔ mile below South Laguna. Private beach.

Matt Kivlin faces a husky section at SALT CREEK, *circa* 1950. [Joe Quigg]

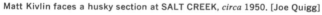

Salt Creek. (1) South Point. (2) The Falls. (3) Beach surf. North Point is out of sight at left. Surf at the Falls is about 6 feet. (A) Highway 101. (B) Entrance road.

SALT CREEK—There are four areas.

- SOUTH POINT—Near rocky point at south end of beach, lines build outside and produce a very fast peak takeoff which runs into a left lineup that is fast but still allows much turning. Breaks very hard when large, and occasionally reaches 15 feet. Short fast rights possible in smaller surf. Wave has best shape on south swell, but not all south swells break here. Best at medium tide; lower tides increase number of sections, higher tides number of bowls. Blown out by west winds, but kelp and Dana Point protect area somewhat from south winds. Submerged rocks inside takeoff point are a hazard to people as well as boards. Rest of beach sandy except at high tides. Upcoast current when surf is big. Hard to paddle out on a big day; easiest places are in channel just north of break or from point between sets (lots of luck!).

- THE FALLS—Winter sometimes brings up a beach-type peak about two-thirds of the way to the point from the entrance gate. North swell, but inconsistent. Usually a right. Must be 6-8 feet to break, can reach 15. Low tide best. Beach sandy. May be up when many other places are flat.

- THE BEACH—Surf appears all along the beach; these shifting peaks are hard to wire: some wall up; others mush out.

- NORTH POINT—A right. Rocks demolish boards. Must be 8 feet to be safely ridable.

Turn off Highway 101 one mile north of Dana Point. Beach is privately owned. As of Summer 1963 Salt Creek is being operated by the United States Surfing Association—the first such beach in California. The area near the South Point is reserved for surfing. Entrance is for USSA members showing membership cards; each member is allowed one guest. Fee is 25 cents per surfer, and the proceeds are used to pay the lifeguard required by Orange County law and to keep up the beach. In winter, when a lifeguard is neither required nor present, the beach is run privately and an entrance charge of 75 cents is paid at the gate, the money being deposited in a tin-cup-on-a-stick extended over the fence by the caretaker.* Restrooms and parking area on beach.

*It is reported that tin cup has been replaced by clothespin.

DANA STRAND—Inconsistent and poor shorebreak below and in front of private property.

DANA POINT—view from the pergola on the cliff. [Greg MacGillivray]

Flying surfboard, typifying usual DANA POINT confusion when the surf comes up, fails to faze "Flippy" Hoffman and Renny Yater. [Bruce Brown]

DANA POINT—There are three spots.

- Thick lines wind around the point and build up on outside reefs, with fast takeoff on larger swells (6 to 12-15 feet) developing into a slower, mushier, but often well-shaped lineup. On smaller swells the inside lineup provides good fun-surf at lower tides. Dana is mainly a south-swell spot; it breaks less often in winter—swell must then be big. At higher tides waves are still flatter and mushier; best at low tide, when lineup is faster and more challenging. Ride from the point past the pier to the beach, possible in larger surf, is about 500 yards. Surf inside cove is protected by the point from usual west sea breeze, but takeoff area may be more choppy. Blown out easily by south winds.

    Best takeoff spot is outside near large rocks, but surfer is then in front of rock-strewn point, the danger to board and rider being obvious. Also present here is large sharp kelp-covered rock which forms a turbulent boil at medium and high tides and becomes an obstacle at low tide. Pier is a menace only on larger swells, when lineup extends beyond it; surfers are supposed to stay 100 yards from the pier. Rips seldom occur, but in larger surf a downcoast current develops which is usually not strong enough to impede swimming but can, with the assistance of wind, carry board almost out of sight.

- During smaller surf and at lower tides a very flat peak appears directly out from the pier as a separate surfing spot. Being exceedingly slow and often backing off before reaching shore it is an excellent place for beginners, for one can ride straight off here for about 200 yards. West swell may break here larger than at the point.

- Peaks farther south are seldom ridden, being rather inaccessible. Paddle down from Dana or up from Doheny.

Turn off Highway 101 at north end of city of Dana Point. Surfing always allowed. San Clemente city lifeguard from 10 AM to 6 PM on pier daily in summer, weekends in winter. Also on pier are water fountain and snack shop. Free parking area, restrooms, outdoor shower. Beach closes at midnight. Small-boat harbor to be constructed in Dana Cove will probably put an end to this popular surfing spot or greatly alter its surf.

DANA POINT, Whee! [Bruce Brown]

Doheny. (1) Main break. (2) Garbage Hole. Surf is about 2 feet. Forty surfers are in the water. (A) Highway 101-Alternate. (B) "True" Highway 101. (C) Town of Capistrano Beach. (D) San Juan River.

Little waves display good quality when held up by an offshore wind at DANA POINT.

[John McChristy]

DOHENY BEACH STATE PARK—There are two areas.

- Main break consists of long lines that peak up in several places, allowing takeoffs in both directions. South end of line is a right and provides longest rides, but lefts are often less crowded. Usually mushy waves are even more so at high tide; best at lower tides, though extreme low is again poor.

- GARBAGE HOLE (BONEYARD, SEWER, INDICATOR)—300 yards north and outside the main break, large rocks protrude from the water. At higher tides short fast rights are found here.

Waves are rarely over 5 feet. Though easy-breaking, lineup is well-shaped and allows both nose-riding and turning. Area takes both north and south swells, with former usually better. Bottom is cobblestones and sand with a few larger rocks; beach is sandy with scattered rocks. No strong currents. Doheny is physically one of the best learning spots on the coast, but the water is crowded with up to 200 surfers, many of whom do not even try to hold on to their boards after a wipeout, endangering everyone.

Location: on Highway 101 between Dana Point and Capistrano Beach. Overnight camping permitted here – this is the first public beach campground south of Arroyo Sequit. Camping costs $1 per car; party must include "responsible adult." Usual waiting list a week long in summer; ask park ranger for details on reserving a campsite. Surfers are requested to stay out of camping area unless actually camping. Fifty cents is charged when car enters park. Restrooms, showers, gas burners for cooking all provided. Entry only from 8 AM to 12 midnight in summer, 8 AM to 10 PM in winter. Snack bar open during daytime. Lifeguard on duty daily. Surfing any time north of San Juan River; no surfing south of it.

Discipline problem posed to state park administrators by hundreds of gremlins brings frequent threat of closing area to surfing—for park's importance for camping is even greater than for surfing. Planned jetty if built may change break somewhat, as may Dana Point Harbor.

KILLER CAPO (CAPISTRANO BEACH PIER)—Reef one pier's-length beyond end of Capistrano Beach Pier breaks on west swell. Must be 6 feet to break, can pass 15. Wave usually pops up from nowhere and dies away just as fast: a vertical takeoff followed by a turn right or left, and then nothing (unless surf is huge, when ride to beach is possible). Low tide best. Access is from south end of Doheny park—beach directly in front is private.

THE BARGE—300 yards south of Killer Capo west swell brings up fair peak over sunken barge about even with the end of pier. Low tide best. Private beach.

DODY'S REEF—Peak appears occasionally on big west swell ½ mile south of Killer Capo and ¼ mile or more from shore. Lefts better than rights.

POCHE—On larger swells lines build on reefs far outside into occasionally makable waves with long rides. Outside waves are flat and hard to paddle into: it is usually necessary to go straight off for some distance before turning. Never breaks hard. Lower tides preferred. Takes any swell. Inside peaks make good fun-surf and are occasionally fast. Best spot is just north of main area, at end of row of beach homes. Medium tides best. West swell preferred. Area blown out by westerly winds, but offshore winds improve surf greatly. Beach and bottom sandy. Rips and strong currents infrequent. Location: 1 mile north of San Clemente. Parking area across Highway 101 at corner of Camino Capistrano. Beach access via pedestrian underpass. No lifeguard. Area private.

THE SIGN—Beach surf like Poche's breaks half a mile farther south and a little farther out. Private property.

(1) Riffraff Reef. (2) The Depot. (A) Highway 101. (B) El Camino Real. (C) San Clemente.

RIFFRAFF REEF—Peaks break in front of San Clemente Trailer Park a half mile north of the Depot.

THE DEPOT (TRAIN STATION)—In front of San Clemente train depot at north end of town is beach surf. Best spot is near tiny pier. Rights and lefts. Medium-high tide preferred. San Clemente City lifeguard on duty 10 AM to 6 PM daily in summer. Cafe nearby. Fire rings on beach.

Joe Daley, SAN CLEMENTE PIER. [John Fowler]

San Clemente. (1) Pier. (2) Sometime Reef. (3) Trafalgar Lane, with surf about 4 feet. (4) The Canyon. (A) Highway 101.

Joe Metzger, SAN CLEMENTE PIER. [John Fowler]

GUMU (NORTH REEF)—Located 600 yards from shore and 600 yards north of San Clemente Pier. Rocks exposed; takes big swell to be safely ridable.

SAN CLEMENTE PIER—Swells build up on sandbars into good two-way beach break peaks on either side of pier. Line-up is occasionally well-shaped and nearly always fast. Good nose-rides. Good fun-surf up to 5 feet. Occasionally good when larger during day-after-storm surf. Breaks on all swells but peaky winter surf is best. Large south swells close out. Best on medium-high tide. Blown out by most westerly winds. Waves become very hollow during offshore winds. Beach and bottom both sandy. Only danger is barnacle-covered pier pilings. No rips or strong currents when ridable. San Clemente City lifeguard headquarters is on pier; guards on duty 10 AM to 6 PM year round. Fire rings on beach. Cafes, market nearby. All-day surfing area north of pier is marked by buoys. Metered parking near pier. City police are very conscientious. A few gremlins and many vacationing marines.

SOMETIME REEF—Sometimes breaks.

TRAFALGAR LANE (T STREET, THE OVERPASS)—Swells peak up far outside and form waves ridable in both directions. Waves often hard to paddle into, as they may elusively rise up and then flatten out, not breaking till beach. Occasionally well-shaped fast peaks. Consistently over 3 feet. Closes out at 8 feet. Breaks on all swells. Best at lower tides, when waves are faster and easier to get into. Good only when completely glassy. Blown out easily by south wind, but west wind may take a little longer. Beach and bottom both sandy. Rips and strong currents present during sizable surf. Location: 1/3 mile south of San Clemente Pier, at foot of Avenida Esplanade. Free parking lot by pedestrian overpass leading to beach. City lifeguard 10 AM to 6 PM in summer.

THE CANYON (PALISADES)—Typical beach surf slightly better in front of gully one quarter mile south of the Overpass. No surfing 10 AM to 6 PM in summer.

THE RIVIERA—Very good hollow fast yet makable beach surf. Location: 4/10 mile below the Canyon and just north of San Clemente Beach State Park. It too is in front of a canyon; park on its south side and walk through tunnel under train track to beach. No surfing 10 AM to 6 PM in summer.

SAN CLEMENTE BEACH STATE PARK—Fair beach surf seems to be a little better in front of the two lifeguard towers. Camping permitted, $1 per car. Entry into park costs 50 cents per car. Surfing allowed all day though areas may be restricted when beach is crowded. Location: 1 mile south of City of San Clemente.

(1) Cotton's Point breaks farther out than this; it isn't really up today. (2) Larry's Place. (3) Upper Trestle. (4) Lower Trestle. Surf visible here is about 4 - 5 feet. (5) Gung Ho Shores. (6) Church. (7) San Onofre. (A) Highway 101. (B) Basilone Road. (C) Railroad track. (D) San Mateo Creek.

COTTON'S POINT (SAN MATEO POINT)—Long swells build into well-formed lefts and frequently good rights on summer swells; rarely breaks in winter. Ridable over 3 feet, but excellent quality comes only with larger south swells (6-15 feet), when takeoffs are fast and exclusively left lineup is almost vertical and extremely well-shaped. Surf over 8 feet breaks on reef farther from shore, so beware the outside set! Wave breaks hard—is not usually tubular, but comes down all at once. Best at medium tide. Blown out by any south wind; west wind takes a little longer. Occasional rips and parallel currents on larger swells. Beach sandy. Main danger to boards is shorebreak, which has been known to slam boards sandward with enough force to break them in half. In bigger surf paddle out north of break. Cotton's is in front of privately owned property which serves as good refuge from Marines in case of pursuit from adjoining Trestles area. At present, direct access is forbidden; paddling or walking below mean high tide line from San Clemente Beach State Park, one mile north, is legal.

LARRY'S PLACE—Surf between Cotton's Point and Upper Trestle is sometimes ridable and may provide welcome solitude.

UPPER TRESTLE—Along this beach large peaks move in, the best of which are just south of railroad trestle over San Mateo Creek. Smaller waves permit good nose-riding and turning. Over 6 feet waves are thick and hard to paddle into early; late fast takeoff becomes necessary and hot lineup develops. Waves this size break very hard and pushing through them can be difficult and tiring if you are caught inside. Size reaches 12 feet. Breaks on most swells, but north and west far superior. Smaller swells best at lower tides, while larger ones take medium tide. Blown out by south wind easily, by west wind eventually; offshore winds make waves faster. Beach is sandy with sharp rocks beginning near water's edge. Sharp snails and mussel shells increase likelihood of cut feet. Rips and strong currents during larger surf. Beware the outside set!

The Trestles (both Upper and Lower) are located in front of Camp Pendleton Marine Corps Reservation. Trespassing is forbidden, and imagination is necessary to gain entry (walking 1½ miles from San Clemente Beach State Park is considered quite pedestrian). Detection can potentially result in $500 fine and imprisonment; but usual action is merely expulsion from the area, occasional interrogation, name-taking, temporary confiscation of surfboard, and other petty displays of imagined authority by enlisted underlings. Camping not recommended due to mosquitoes and possibility of being run over by night patrol jeep. Even as the United States Surfing Association and the San Onofre Surfing Club negotiate with the USMC to make more direct access legal, guerrilla warfare continues.*

* Warning: as this book goes to press it is reported that in recent weeks the Marines—perhaps subverted by a conspiracy aimed at thwarting the President's physical fitness program—have been pursuing surfers with unusual vigah. More importantly, arrested trespassers have been subjected to exceedingly vigorous fines.

Phil Edwards, COTTON'S POINT. [Bruce Brown]

Ladies first: a surfer pulls out to let Marge Calhoun speed by at COTTON'S POINT.
[Bruce Brown]

Phil Stubbs, UPPER TRESTLE. [Bruce Brown]

(1) West swell at Lower Trestle. Lefts from here look good, but rights run into sections. For rights, peak farther south appears more promising. (2) Gung-Ho Shores. (A) Highway 101. (B) Basilone Road. (C) Railroad track.

LOWER TRESTLE—Long swells peak just south of point and create some of the best surf in Southern California, with long fast rides. Mostly rights, but shorter fast lefts sometimes of equal quality. Waves are thick and hard to paddle into early; late takeoffs frequently necessary. Waves hold up long enough for long fade into hook before dropping to bottom, turning just ahead of break, and shooting across wall—after which good turning, climbing-and-dropping, etc., are possible sometimes for 300 yards. Consistently 4-6 feet, frequently larger, occasionally up to 12 feet. Breaks on most swells, but extreme south swells far superior. Medium tide best. Blown out by south winds easily, by west winds after a while. Occasional rips and strong south currents develop during larger surf. Beach is sandy with rocks beginning at mean high tide line and extending seaward. Snails, sharp rocks, and sea urchins are hazards to boards and feet. Distance from shore is considerable, and poor swimmers may encounter trouble struggling shoreward while being pounded by hard-breaking waves and negotiating strong currents present when surf is big.

Location: ⅓ mile below Upper Trestle. Access problem same as for Upper Trestle. (See page 165.)

"Bosco" Burns, UPPER TRESTLE. [Bruce Brown]

GUNG HO SHORES—Between Lower Trestle and Church is nearly a mile of beach where illegal right slides can be found.

CHURCH—Lines wind around from Trestles area and rise to form a long peak or wall that holds up long enough to be easily makable, then runs into a hot lineup inside. Breaks very hard over five feet and resembles Trestles wave. Under three feet waves are usually mushy. Breaks on all swells but good only on north or west swell. Waves have best shape and break hardest at medium tide. Blown out by south and west winds. Light offshore winds make waves break harder, but best when completely glassy. Sandy beach, rock bottom. Occasional rips during large swells.

Location: on Camp Pendleton Marine Base at mouth of San Onofre Creek, in front of church where road to San Onofre surfing beach first reaches ocean. This area is off-limits for all surfers, including those in the San Onofre Surfing Club. Access is (illegally) attained by walking in 300 yards from Highway 101 (no-parking area) or by driving in to San Onofre with a member of the club and "stopping off on the way." Obviously we cannot recommend either method.

San Onofre. Surf 3-4 feet. Large number of ridable peaks provides room for many surfers. White water from "The Point" is visible at far left.

SAN ONOFRE—There are three different kinds of surf here.

- OUTSIDE—In several places swell builds 200-400 yards from shore into thick peaks which hold up long; surfers not used to such waves find them hard to paddle into because they are so flat. Surfer in correct position, however, can get fast takeoff in either direction; remainder of ride is usually slow and mushy—the epitome of lazy fun-surf, with much turning possible and even several complete changes of direction on a single wave. Not overly challenging; good learning spot, enjoyable for anyone. Best at incoming lower tides. Best size 4-8 feet, at which size some of the lineups are well-shaped. Takes most swells, with south preferred.
- INSIDE—Shorebreak is smaller, faster and good for hot-dogging. Medium tide best.
- THE POINT—One-quarter mile north of main area. Long lineups. Hollower and steeper than outside surf at main beach. Sometimes makable, sometimes not. Takes west swell best.

Area is blown out by south and west winds. Offshore wind improves outside surf especially. Beach sandy with small rocks extending into water; larger pebbles sometimes damage loose boards, but often boards lost outside are found floating in calm water. Rips infrequent and currents weak.

Location: 4 miles below San Clemente. San Onofre is only beach on Camp Pendleton Marine Corps Base which is available to anyone outside the military. Entry is possible only to the 800 members of the San Onofre Surfing Club, their family and personal guests. Members leave Highway 101 at Basilone Road, stop at USMC sentry who checks to see if car bears current sticker and often asks for membership card. Rest rooms on beach, but no food or water.

Camp Pendleton Marine Base. View southward from near San Onofre. Excellent beach surf extends as far as the eye can see, protected from surfer invasions by the United States Marine Corps.

CAMP PENDLETON AREA—Fifteen miles of ocean front between San Onofre and Oceanside has ridable beach surf all along. The average quality of this surf is very good—like that of Oceanside, Encinitas and Del Mar farther south. Waves tend to be thick, sometimes mushy but frequently well-shaped. Here and there are flat reefs which produce consistently located peaks that break a little farther out than surf along nearby beaches. Two of these are **MILE ZERO** (1 mile south of San Onofre) and **GULLY HOLE** (2 miles.farther south). At no place does the surf break as far out as at San Onofre; at no place are there rides consistently as long as at Lower Trestle, though quality at some spots compares. As is well known, the US Marine Corps does not permit use of these beaches by the public, and till recently surfers have rarely been motivated to sneak in here as they have in the Trestles area. So for the most part this section of coast is *terra incognita.*

171

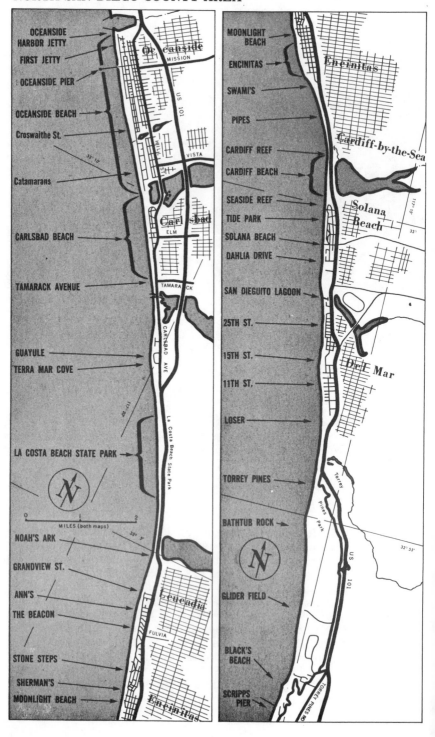

OCEANSIDE HARBOR JETTY
FIRST JETTY
OCEANSIDE PIER
OCEANSIDE BEACH
Croswaithe St.
Catamarans
CARLSBAD BEACH
TAMARACK AVENUE
GUAYULE
TERRA MAR COVE
LA COSTA BEACH STATE PARK
NOAH'S ARK
GRANDVIEW ST.
ANN'S
THE BEACON
STONE STEPS
SHERMAN'S
MOONLIGHT BEACH

MOONLIGHT BEACH
ENCINITAS
SWAMI'S
PIPES
CARDIFF REEF
CARDIFF BEACH
SEASIDE REEF
TIDE PARK
SOLANA BEACH
DAHLIA DRIVE
SAN DIEGUITO LAGOON
25TH ST.
15TH ST.
11TH ST.
LOSER
TORREY PINES
BATHTUB ROCK
GLIDER FIELD
BLACK'S BEACH
SCRIPPS PIER

Oceanside
MISSION
US 101
VISTA
Carlsbad
ELM
TAMARACK
CARLSBAD AVE
La Costa Beach State Park
MILES (both maps)
0   2
Leucadia
FULVIA
Encinitas

Encinitas
Cardiff-by-the-Sea
Solana Beach
Del Mar
Torrey Pines Park
US 101
32° 55'

NORTH SAN DIEGO COUNTY AREA

Sandy beaches are found along nearly all of the coast, with good beach surf that breaks 50-200 yards from shore. There are also a number of reef breaks, a pier and a point. Area is under-used and can support many more surfers than it presently has; uncrowded waves are always available unless everything is blown out. Problem in many places is descending steep palisades to beach. Towns, from north to south: Oceanside, Carlsbad, Leucadia, Encinitas, Cardiff-by-the-Sea, Solana Beach, and Del Mar, after which Highway 101 heads inland toward downtown San Diego. Campground (only one in San Diego County) is at La Costa Beach State Park, between Carlsbad and Leucadia; charge is $1 per car.

OCEANSIDE HARBOR JETTY—Peak breaks over sandbar just below south jetty of Oceanside Harbor. Rights preferred because lefts head into jetty, which is then a hazard. Good on a west swell. It is understood that the lefts on the north side of this jetty have been destroyed by dredging; surfing inside the harbor is illegal anyhow.

FIRST JETTY—Peak breaks over sandbar formed by jetty between the harbor and the pier. Takes most swells.

Bob Betz leans on air as he turns into this wave at Croswaithe Street in OCEANSIDE.
[Don Gilliam]

Oceanside Pier. No surf today. Lagoon on beach just south of pier, brought about by pumping of sand from Oceanside Harbor, is temporary. (A) Highway 101, running through city of Oceanside.

OCEANSIDE PIER—Waves peaking on both sides of pier offer rides in both directions. Best on smaller swells; in surf over six feet peaks join and waves close out. North side of pier can sometimes handle a bigger swell (mainly lefts). Breaks on all swells, with peakier swells ridable at larger size. Shape best at higher tides. Area blows out easily. Only hazard is pier; currents can pull lost boards into pier, and barnacles are sharp.

Metered parking just south of pier, where surfing is allowed all day. Restaurant there too. City lifeguard headquarters just north of pier on beach. Guards on duty 10 AM to 6 PM.

OCEANSIDE—On glassy mornings you can enter the water practically anywhere and find well-shaped beach tubes. The area takes most swells. With an even swell waves over 4-5 feet become unmakable, while a peaky swell permits waves to be ridden up to 6-8 feet. The bottom is currently in a state of flux because of sand being pumped in from Oceanside Harbor.

About a mile south of the pier the locals single out these spots (from north to south): SHORT STREET, CROSWAITHE STREET, THE DUNES (at the mouth of Loma Alta Creek), BUCCANEER HOTEL, CASSIDY STREET, and CATAMARANS, but the waves here differ little from those elsewhere along the beach.

CARLSBAD—A mile of beach surf between Buena Vista Lagoon and Tamarack Avenue resembles that of Oceanside.

174

Tamarack Avenue (A) connects with Hightway 101 (B) in Carlsbad. Surf today appears better about two blocks north; size is 3-4 feet. (C) Carlsbad Avenue. (D) Agua Hedionda.

TAMARACK AVENUE (CARLSBAD BEACH STATE PARK)—Thick waves build outside over reef into peaks with rights and lefts of equal quality. Much turning is possible, as waves line up and flatten out according to bottom contours. Good nose-riding conditions infrequent. Breaks on all swells, but best in a southwest or when no single swell direction predominates. Ridable up to 8 feet, at which size the wave sections— especially on rights. Best at low to medium tide. Blown out by south and west winds. A few rocks near shore.

Location: in Carlsbad on Carlsbad Avenue, three streets north of Agua Hedionda Lagoon. Surfing area is flagged during crowded season. Lifeguard on duty in summer 10 AM to 6 PM. Snack bar across street. Restrooms and fire pits at beach.

A little boy on a little wave — Pete Johnson, OCEANSIDE. [Don Gilliam]

(1) Guayule. (2) Terra Mar Cove. Surf is 5-6 feet. (A) Terra Mar community. (B) Carlsbad. (C) Agua Hedionda. (D) Carlsbad Avenue. (E) Highway 101. (F) Encina Power Plant.

GUAYULE (TERRA MAR POINT, ENCINA POWER PLANT)—Peak 400 yards out from the private community of Terra Mar breaks at 6 to 12 feet; smaller surf is very ordinary beach break. Waves are thickish peaks with better lefts than rights. Low tide preferred. Best on south swell. Kelp offers only minor protection from onshore winds. Public must park half a mile north of break, near south side of Agua Hedionda Lagoon, and walk down.

TERRA MAR COVE—Reef a couple hundred yards south of Guayule breaks from 3 to 12 feet in winter. Rights and lefts. Low tide preferred. Blown out easily. Access problem same as for Guayule.

LA COSTA BEACH STATE PARK—Quite ordinary beach break with good shape now and then. No major hazards. Blown out by south and west winds. This is the only beach campground between San Clemente and the Mexican border. Price, $1 per night per car. Often crowded in summer. Lifeguard on duty June-September. Location: between Carlsbad and Leucadia on Highway 101.

LEUCADIA—Good beach surf breaks all along Leucadia's two miles of ocean front. The following spots are surfed more often because they allow easy descent to the beach from atop high cliffs. From north to south:

- NOAH'S ARK TRAILER PARK—Ordinary beach break. Market and cafe on highway. Located at Batiquitos Lagoon just north of town.

- GRANDVIEW STREET—Outside reef produces beach-type break on any swell but is best on a south. Ridable from 2 to 10 feet, but surf under 3-4 feet is shorebreak only. Good fun-surf from 4 to 6 feet; larger surf is faster, sometimes unmakable. Trail descends cliff from vacant lot. Beach is under San Diego County jurisdiction.

- ANN'S—Peaks at foot of Jason Street, but no access here; paddle over from The Beacon.

- THE BEACON—Much like Grandview Street, in that outside breaks become good at 5-8 feet. An easy break. Peak just south of parking lot behaves more like reef at times than other nearby breaks. Restaurants close by. No facilities. Located at foot of Fulvia Street.

- STONE STEPS (PONTO BEACH STATE PARK)—Another easy access route to Leucadia's uncrowded beach peaks. Located at foot of South El Portal Street.

- SHERMAN'S—At foot of La Mesa Street. Dirt trail descends cliff at south corner of vacant lot.

Lifeguards patrol area by jeep.

GRANDVIEW STREET in Leucadia. A glassy wave for Eric Schultz. [Don Gilliam]

MOONLIGHT BEACH STATE PARK—Waves form into typically fast beach-break-type lefts and rights on smaller swells. Locals speak of peaks as "Mooney's Lefts," "Mooney Mooney," and "Honey Mooney." Can break hard for size. Occasionally good fun-surf, good nose-rides, but little turning. Usually closes out over 6-8 feet. Breaks on all swells, summer being best. Favors medium tide. Blown out by westerly and southerly winds. Sandy beach and bottom. Strong currents rare.

Lifeguard on duty 9 AM to 5 PM in winter, 9 AM to 6 PM in summer in main headquarters located on beach at foot of "B" Street, Encinitas. Surfing areas are designated by lifeguards, depending on crowds. Some part of beach is always reserved for surfing. Dressing rooms, stoves, fire pits, snack bar all on beach.

ENCINITAS—Good beach surf continues south of Moonlight Beach though it is mostly inaccessible (except by walking from Moonlight) because of high cliffs.

(1) Swami's, breaking sloppily at about 4 feet. (2) Inaccessible beach surf below Encinitas is 5-6 feet.

Little John, big wave, SWAMI'S. "L. J." Richards stalls slightly, playing it as close to the line as possible. The goofy-foot behind him is preparing to prone out one heck of a lot of soup.
[Don Gilliam]

SWAMI'S (SEACLIFF ROADSIDE PARK)—South of point lines build over reefs into beautiful peaks offering good rights and frequent lefts on smaller swells. With larger surf (7 - 15 feet) lefts close out and right lineup becomes very hot, frequently hollow, yet allowing excellent turning; takeoffs then are straight-up-and-down. Inside break known locally as "Malcolm's Reef" is another peak takeoff on small swells; on larger swells it's a hot section. Breaks summer and winter, but south swell usually very mushy and sectiony. Immeasurably better on winter swells. Normally best at medium-low tide; high tide makes waves mushy and hard to paddle into. Blows out on south wind but somewhat protected from west winds by cove and kelp. Rips infrequent but as surf is frequently large in winter, currents do develop.

Main danger to the inexperienced is distance from shore, but bottom inside is shallow. Sand extends up to small rocks and cliff, the latter comprising main danger to boards at higher tides. However, lost boards usually pop up before running entire distance to beach. Long, flat submerged shale strata inside offer negligible danger. More than 15 surfers make area feel crowded, but 40 or more in the water is not unusual.

Location: at south end of Encinitas, adjacent to Self-Realization Foundation property, which is easily identified from Highway 101 by gold mosque-like domes. Park at top of 129 wooden stairs leading down cliff to beach. San Diego County lifeguards from June to September. Local surfers have established good relations with the Self-Realization Foundation, and visitors to this well-known surfing spot are expected to cooperate. Cheap and excellent food of the vegetarian variety, including "mushroom-burgers" and "Indian dahi drink," is sold at SRF's restaurant on Highway 101 near parking area. Camping, including parking overnight in cars, is absolutely forbidden; park caretaker is deputized to arrest violators.

SWAMI'S presents... "John's Other Wave." Will he make that inside section? The surfer paddling over and another sitting outside are tuned in to learn the outcome of this exciting episode. Note the similarity between this wave and the slightly larger one on the previous page. Knowledgeable surfers examining a picture can often tell where it was taken by the appearance of the wave alone. [Don Gilliam]

SWAMI'S from the cliff during a medium-sized north swell. [Leroy Grannis]

SWAMI'S—home-town surf for Rusty Miller. [Lee Peterson]

Cardiff Reef. A dozen surfers can be seen paddling out in the channel south of the peak as the first wave of a 5-foot set breaks outside. Cardiff beach surf is to right. (A) Town of Cardiff-by-the-Sea. (B) Highway 101.

PIPES—Peaks offer rights and lefts at any tide. Area stays glassy because of kelp outside. No hazards. Best on southwest swell. Location: ⅔ mile below Swami's. Parking along cliff; trail descends to beach. Patrolled by lifeguard jeep from Cardiff.

CARDIFF REEF—Swells bounce off reefs outside to form good two-way peaks which build and hold up a long time before breaking. Break is usually gentle. Lineup is well-formed but seldom fast—lefts generally faster than rights. Closes out at about 8 feet. Blows out easily on south wind, but stays glassy longer than most nearby places on west wind due to kelp outside. Best on west swell, when waves break hardest and are well-shaped. Tide makes little difference. Beach is sandy, bottom shale and sand—few hazards. San Diego County lifeguard on duty 10 AM to 6 PM during warmer months. Parking area just off Highway 101 next to beach.

CARDIFF-BY-THE-SEA—Beach surf at mouth of San Elijo Lagoon, south of Cardiff Reef, can accommodate overflow crowds from nearby reef breaks. Locals single out surf in front of the BEACH BARN and the BEACON INN.

Paws on the schnozz, CARDIFF REEF. [Peter Rae]

(1) Seaside Reef. (2) Tide Park. City in background is Solana Beach.

SEASIDE REEF—Big hollow shifting peak allows good rights and excellent lefts. Any swell OK; best chance of high quality on a south swell. Any tide good. Light onshore winds are foiled by kelp, but persistent sea breeze eventually blows out the surf. Occasional rips. Beach is private, belonging to Seaside Motel and Trailer Park, but owners permit surfers to use beach if they avoid swimmers (surfing area is flagged). Location: just north of Solana Beach, just south of San Elijo Lagoon. Park north of trailer park. Nearest lifeguard is at Cardiff.

TIDE PARK (SOLANA COVE, TABLE TOP)—Wide peak breaks 300 yards out over flat table-like ledge. Rights and lefts, with latter better. Must be 5 feet to break well. Comes up on any swell, but a well-lined-up south is best. Outgoing tide preferred. Can reach 10-12 feet and still be ridable. Kelp protects area from light onshore winds. Submerged rocks a hazard, especially at low tide. Public stairway descends cliffs from Solana Vista Road at north end of Solana Beach. San Diego County lifeguard in tower 10 AM to 6 PM in summer.

SEASIDE REEF. View from cliff just south of trailer park. [Doug Erickson]

SOLANA BEACH COUNTY PARK—Submerged outside reefs form consistent beach-break-type lefts and rights ridable up to 5 or 6 feet, at which size surf breaks hard. Past this size peaks usually join to produce a single unridable wall. Usually get-up-and-go waves, but occasional rare form allows climbing-and-dropping, etc. Breaks summer and winter, with peaky winter surf best. Also good with glassy day-after-storm surf. At high tide waves break close to cliff and are made bumpy by backwash; best at medium tide. Not blown out easily except by southerly winds.

Location: At foot of Plaza Street in center of Solana Beach. San Diego County lifeguard headquarters is here; guards 10 AM to dark year round. They designate surfing area by signs. Rule enforced strictly to protect swimmers. Dressing rooms, snack bars, restaurants nearby.

SOUTH SOLANA BEACH—Beach surf extends southward from Solana Beach Park for a mile. Area is never crowded because descent of cliffs to beach is difficult in most places. Two convenient access points are:

- DAHLIA DRIVE—At foot of Dahlia Drive, at south end of populated part of Solana Beach, dirt road leads to trail down cliff.
- SAN DIEGUITO LAGOON—1 mile south of town, where Highway 101 again descends to sea level.

SOLANA BEACH. Bob Cramer points where he's going and trims his board to get there.
[Doug Erickson]

Del Mar. (1) Fifteenth Street. (2) Eleventh Street. On land: (A) Highway 101. (B) Railroad track. (C) Fifteenth Street.

DEL MAR—Ridable peaks break all along Del Mar's three miles of beach. Spots singled out by locals (from north to south):

- 25TH STREET—Ordinary beach break; surfing area sometimes designated by lifeguards, depending on crowds.
- 15TH STREET (DEL MAR PIER)—The pier is gone but the name lingers on. Peak forms over rock bottom somewhat farther out than along rest of beach; takeoff is followed by usually well-formed left or right lineup. Wave does not break very hard, begins to close out at 8 feet. Breaks all year round but better on south swell. Concession stand at 17th Street. Free parking lot (very bumpy) owned by Del Mar Hotel may be closed, but parking on street is OK.
- 11TH STREET—Another peak much like 15th Street but not as good. Park on street. Steep trail descends cliff.
- THE LOSER—Inaccessible peak in front of canyon at south end of town is often what its name implies.

Area is protected somewhat from west winds by heavy kelp outside, but south winds blow out everything. San Diego County lifeguards on duty 10 AM to 6 PM in summer at 25th and 17th Streets.

Bathtub Rock in Torrey Pines Beach State Park. Surf is blown out, but peak is evident. Note absence of roads of any sort and curious formation of cliffs. A queer place indeed.

TORREY PINES STATE PARK—Fair beach surf lines 4½ miles of state-owned ocean frontage. Even the easily accessible portions are seldom crowded, while the parts farther from roads are hardly ever surfed. Surfing is generally permitted everywhere though on busy days near the lifeguard tower (2 miles south of Del Mar) certain zones may be flagged. Isolated strand farther south is locally referred to as "Queer Beach," undoubtedly because of the odd waves encountered there. In front of BATHTUB ROCK (FLAT ROCK) in this area is a submerged point with consistently located rights and lefts (lefts better). Still farther south, beach can be reached by trail down cliff from road to GLIDER FIELD just south of golf course. Area is located between Del Mar and La Jolla. Lifeguards, who patrol only near the guard tower, are on duty from 10 AM to 6 PM daily in summer, weekends in late spring and early fall, and not at all from October to April. Snack wagon sometimes. No camping.

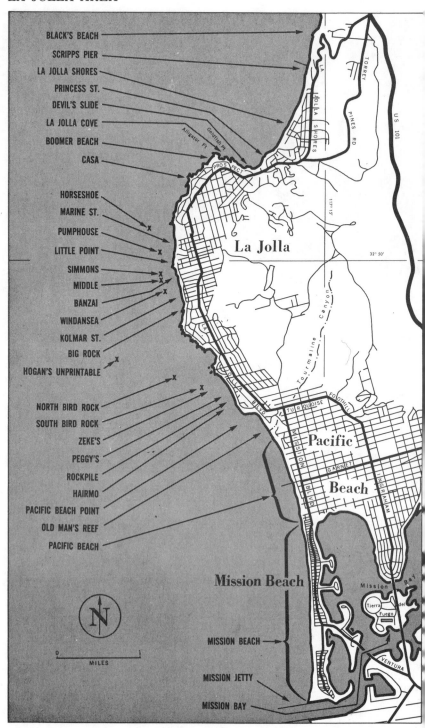

BLACK'S BEACH
SCRIPPS PIER
LA JOLLA SHORES
PRINCESS ST.
DEVIL'S SLIDE
LA JOLLA COVE
BOOMER BEACH
CASA

HORSESHOE
MARINE ST.
PUMPHOUSE
LITTLE POINT
SIMMONS
MIDDLE
BANZAI
WINDANSEA
KOLMAR ST.
BIG ROCK
HOGAN'S UNPRINTABLE

NORTH BIRD ROCK
SOUTH BIRD ROCK
ZEKE'S
PEGGY'S
ROCKPILE
HAIRMO
PACIFIC BEACH POINT
OLD MAN'S REEF
PACIFIC BEACH

MISSION BEACH
MISSION JETTY
MISSION BAY

La Jolla

Pacific

Beach

Mission Beach

N

0   1
MILES

LA JOLLA AREA

This region offers an amazing variety of surf. La Jolla itself is known for its reef breaks, less so for its point surf; while La Jolla Shores to the north and Pacific Beach and Mission Beach to the south present several miles of good beach surf punctuated by two piers and a jetty. Highway 101 lies inland. A tour near the coastline from north to south leaves 101 south of Torrey Pines State Park and follows La Jolla Shores Drive through La Jolla Shores; continues along Torrey Pines Road, Prospect Street, and La Jolla Boulevard through La Jolla proper; and follows Mission Boulevard through Pacific Beach and Mission Beach. Garnet Avenue leads three miles from Highway 101 to Pacific Beach. There is no campground, though rumors are that one may some day be set up in the Mission Bay recreational area.

BLACK'S BEACH—In front of small rocky point-like jog in coastline is typical beach surf up to 5-6 feet, but larger surf breaks on outside reefs and reaches 12 feet. Best on a north swell, also breaks on a west. Location: just north of La Jolla. Half-mile walk along beach from public parking lot (25 cents) north of Scripps Institute. Direct access through fenced-off private property is permitted only on an individual basis by owner.

Eric Murphy and his wet-suit tail are outlined against floating foam at LA JOLLA SHORES.
[Garth I. Murphy]

Scripps Pier. Wind-chop can be seen glistening in the sunlight. La Jolla Shores is just to the right of the picture. (A) Scripps Institute of Oceanography. (B) La Jolla Shores Drive.

SCRIPPS PIER AND BEACH—When bottom conditions are right, lines peak up farther out on either side of the pier than along the adjacent beach. On the south side rights are preferred; surf closes out at six feet. North side is usually a left and is choppier due to odd currents. Best on a north swell; only fair on a south. Access is public; surfing is allowed. Location: La Jolla Shores Boulevard 1 mile north of Torrey Pines Road, in front of Scripps Institute of Oceanography.

LA JOLLA SHORES (THE SHORES)—Swells build into beach-break-type peaks usually offering short fast rides in both directions. Waves are sometimes well-shaped and consistently ridable up to 6-7 feet, after which they break along the entire beach in one big wall. Takes winter swells with west slightly superior; south swell poor. Good at any tide except extreme low, when peaks are absent. Unique in that though a beach break it is not easily blown out, for southerly winds blow off the land. West and northwest winds, however, blow onshore. Locals regard The Shores as "Old Faithful" in winter—some sort of wave is almost guaranteed.

Free parking in lot immediately opposite surfing area. Location: at foot of Vallecitos, off La Jolla Shores Drive, 2/3 mile south of Scripps Institute, and 1/2 mile north of Torrey Pines Road. San Diego City lifeguards on duty from 9 AM to 8 PM in summer and from 9 AM to 5 PM in winter. Surfing is allowed everywhere except in official swimming area, which extends from lifeguard station south to Vallecitos. Swimmers are excluded from official surfing area, which runs from lifeguard station north to the seawall. Lifeguards control water traffic at this popular beach with a public address system. Restrooms and dressing facilities provided. Snack wagon sometimes; cafes in nearby commercial district.

PRINCESS STREET—Good small waves (3-6 feet); reef break. Takes winter swell. Shore consists of round boulders about a foot in diameter, like many beaches in Baja California. Location: Off Torrey Pines Road 1/2 mile south of La Jolla Shores Drive.

DEVIL'S SLIDE (THE SLIDES)—Unlike most of La Jolla's reef breaks, this spot has a slow takeoff and a slow ride. Lefts and rights, with rights longer. Breaks from 3 to 8 feet. North swell is best, west is adequate, south doesn't get in at all. Paddle out from Princess Street or from La Jolla Shores boat launching site. Terrible rocks greet lost boards.

Mike Stewart drops through the initial section at LA JOLLA COVE.   ["Walter" of La Jolla]

Looking south over La Jolla. (1) La Jolla Cove (surfless). (2) North Boomer. (3) South Boomer (4) Casa. (5) Horseshoe. Surf is about 6 feet. (A) Prospect Street. (B) Coast Boulevard.

LA JOLLA COVE—Large peak builds on rocky Alligator Point into vertical takeoff followed by well-shaped left lineup that allows much turning during a ride that may be coaxed along for more than half a mile. Only breaks on winter swells and must be 8 feet or larger to ride. Tide has negligible effect in determining quality of waves. Cliff and kelp aid in preserving glassy conditions. Greatest hazard is within thirty yards of takeoff, where unpredictable section is very hard to make. Boards lost here are assured of extensive damage if they hit rocks on the point and complete destruction if trapped in large cave. It is said that few surfers are seen riding their own boards here. Larger waves (up to 15-20 feet) break farther out and are less critical.

Location: In La Jolla on Coast Boulevard off Prospect Street. La Jolla Cove is officially a swimming area (no boards allowed), but when the surf comes up the usually sheltered cove becomes a seething circle of white water, so that you can neither paddle out nor swim to shore here. Instead descend stairway down cliff just east of Goldfish Point or launch from The Shores and after a wipeout expect a long swim through treacherous currents. Only experienced watermen need apply.

Caught inside at La JOLLA COVE Phil Barber says his prayers. [Lee Peterson]

Who knows... what evil... lurks in the hearts of waves? Body-surfers misjudging the BOOMER BEACH shorebreak will find out soon enough! [Lee Peterson]

BOOMER BEACH—There is a surfing spot at each end of the beach and a rip current in the middle. NORTH BOOMER is a right, SOUTH BOOMER a left. Both are reef breaks close to shore with critical takeoffs followed by fast walls. Waves break very hard, top-to-bottom. Winter swells are preferred, especially at North Boomer; South Boomer breaks infrequently. Medium tide produces best rides, for low tide leaves rocks exposed and dangerous, particularly at South Boomer. Cliff protects the area from south winds, and kelp protects it from west winds. The kelp is frequently a bothersome obstacle on takeoffs. The rip in the middle of the beach can defeat even first-rate swimmers. Beach is noted for bodysurfing. Location: on Coast Boulevard off Prospect Street. San Diego City lifeguard on duty in summer.

CASA—Right slide. Winter break. 6 to 12 feet. Frightfully hollow. Large waves break in very shallow water—dangerous and rarely surfed for this reason. High tide essential. Location: foot of Jenner Street, off Prospect Street, south of concrete seawall.

HORSESHOE, ". . . a hollow right slide with a challenging bowl." [Roy Porello]

Danny Diven executes an incomprehensible maneuver just for the hell of it, in the MARINE STREET shorebreak. [Roy Porello]

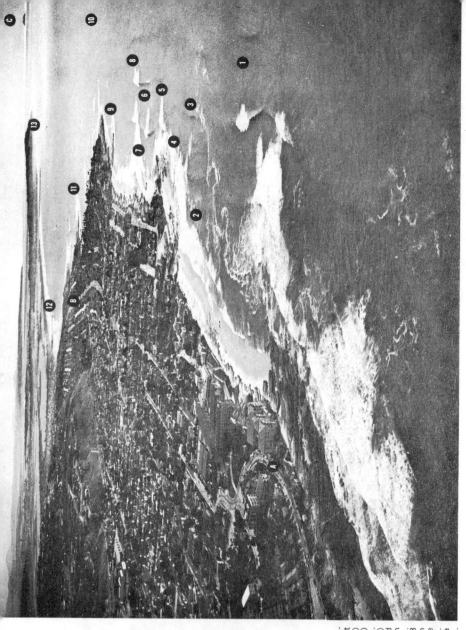

La Jolla. (1) Horseshoe. (2) Marine Street. (3) Pumphouse (not breaking, but swells visible). (4) Little Point. (5) Simmons. (6) Middle. (7) Banzai Shorebreak. (8) Windansea. (9) Big Rock. (10) Hogan's Unprintable. (11) Bird Rock area. (12) Pacific Beach area. (13) Sunset Cliffs area. Surf at Horseshoe is about 8 feet. Swirls of foam between Horseshoe and Pumphouse are caused by a strong rip current. (A) Coast Boulevard. (B) La Jolla Boulevard. (C) Coronado Islands.

HORSESHOE—On a north swell only, this reef offers a very steep takeoff and a hollow right slide with a challenging bowl. Becomes ridable at 6 feet and reaches 15-20. Paddle out about one-quarter mile. Break is slightly north of foot of Marine Street.

MARINE STREET—Has good shorebreak with critical takeoff and hollow right or left slide when surf is under 6 feet. Breaks on all swells but winter best; incoming tide preferred. Location: off La Jolla Boulevard, ⅔ mile north of Windansea (see page 201).

PUMPHOUSE (OUTSIDE MARINE STREET)—Break becomes ridable at 5 feet on any swell, though north and west are best. Left slide preferred when surf is small, while bigger waves break on reefs outside with rights superior. Takeoff is steep. At high tide and just after, shape is best and jagged rocks inside are less hazardous. Location: between Marine Street and Little Point. Park at either.

LITTLE POINT—Point produces thin waves allowing steep takeoffs and short hot hollow lefts. Starts breaking at 2 feet, sections at 8-plus. South swell good, west ridable. All right at any tide but low; best at high tide even in small surf. Rocks inside. One of La Jolla's more consistent summer breaks. Location: At north end of Neptune Place, ¼ mile north of Windansea.

SIMMONS POINT—Reef produces right slide only on 6-to-8-foot west swell. Breaks hard in waist-deep water. Like most of La Jolla's reef breaks, takeoff is steep, ride is hollow, and spot is best on higher tides. Location: south side of Little Point, 300 yards north of Windansea.

MIDDLE—Winter substitute for Windansea starts breaking at 8 feet, gets up to 15 on strong north swell. Thick waves make steep takeoff and hollow ride; rights commoner than lefts. As surf heightens, ride is faster and hollower; and takeoff point moves upcoast, eventually joining Simmons break and destroying possibility of lefts. Top-to-bottom only when huge. Lost boards suffer ravages of rocks. Location: 200 yards north of Windansea.

BANZAI SHOREBREAK—Reef near shore breaks on winter swell (north better than west); right slide is ridable from 4 to 8 feet. As the name suggests, critical takeoffs are followed by waves that suck out and leave unexpecting surfer in midair wondering where the water went. Location: Nautilus Street.

(1) Pumphouse. This is what reef breaks should look like from the air. Surf about 6 feet. (2) Marine Street. (3) Little Point. (A) Marine Street. (B) Neptune Avenue.

WINDANSEA. From top to bottom: John Hayward fades deep into the peak and turns right. [Lee Peterson]   Bill David bends tubeward. [Roy Porello]   Del Cannon swings into a bumpy wave. [Bruce Brown]   Mike Hynson drives through the bowl with a foot on either rail. [Roy Porello]

Looking north over Windansea. (1) Windansea about to break. You can see the white wake left by a surfer taking off on the left side of the peak. Size is about 6 feet. (2) Swells peaking up at Middle. (3) Banzai Shorebreak. (4) Kolmar Street. (5) Big Rock. (6) Pumphouse. (7) Horseshoe. (8) La Jolla Shores. (A) Neptune Avenue. (B) Bonair Street. (C) Nautilus Street.

(1) Windansea: a closer view showing the peak more clearly. (2) Middle. (3) Banzai. (4) Kolmar Street. (A) Neptune Avenue. (B) Bonair Street. (C) Nautilus Street. (D) La Jolla Boulevard.

WINDANSEA—As lines move in, shifting peaks appearing over outside reefs finally form into one concentrated peak which develops into hot left or fair right lineup and ends in grinding shorebreak. Waves break as hard as any on coast and can reach 12-15 feet. Peak must be 4-5 feet to break, but locals measure wave size not by peak but by height of wall that follows (2-3 feet smaller)

Breaks year round but better in summer. Best swell direction is a ."westish" south, when elevator-shaft drop from far side of peak and under it is followed by long fast hollow left slide consummated by a bowl that surprises the neophyte; right slide then is dull. Due south swell produces lefts for purists; take the big drop and a little of the curl, then pull out over the top. On a west swell, go nuts chasing peaks from Windansea to Middle; rights become fairly good, but wipeout on inside reef is harrowing—worse than over-the-falls in the peak. On north swells, surf Middle instead. Windansea is also good with peaky surf the day after a local storm.

Good on any tide. Offshore winds improve shape of wall but are infrequent. Not blown out easily by west wind because of kelp outside, but destroyed by south wind. Strong rips and currents at 8 feet or over, especially "Simmons Rip" on north side of peak. Beach sandy, but shorebreak smashes boards against rocks at higher tides.

Location: at foot of Bonair Street in La Jolla. Often crowded, for more than a dozen persons in the water really trying to catch waves makes surfing uncomfortable. Locals form tight group (though less so than in years past); and alien surfers who get in the way because they don't have the place wired are seldom welcomed here. They are tolerated if they can demonstrate both ability and courtesy in the water. Authorities tend to favor locals in "disputes."

Parking lot in front of break often filled; additional parking on nearby streets. San Diego City lifeguard on duty next to palm-covered shack on beach 9 AM to 8 PM in summer, 9 AM to 5 PM in winter. New comfort stations and change-rooms planned for near future. Windansea (Westbourne Street to Playa del Sur) is designated by city as a surfing area; no swimming is permitted. However, surfers must stay out of official swimming area between Playa del Sur and Palomar Streets.

KOLMAR STREET—A reef near shore 3 blocks south of Windansea. Breaks on south swell, best on west. Rights and lefts. Best at 4 to 6 feet; larger surf closes across to Windansea. Good body-surfing. This is in a swimming area; board-surfing is forbidden and violators of law surf at their own risk.

(1) Big Rock. (A) Palomar Street. (B) La Jolla Boulevard.

BIG ROCK—Point breaks from 2 to 10 feet with straight-up-and-down takeoff and very hollow left slide—the wave spits, and before it does you can see the soup spiraling inside the tube. In smaller surf turning is possible after initial shoot, but at 8 feet entire ride is unbelievably fast. Takes any swell. Breaks with Windansea, but fewer waves per set because smaller waves don't build up as at Windansea. Good at medium or high tide. Main hazard is risk of hitting bottom, for wave breaks in very shallow water. Location: just south of Palomar Street, ½ mile below Windansea. Surfers must stay away from official swimming area near shore which extends northward from Palomar Street.

HOGAN'S UNPRINTABLE (THE DIFFERENTIAL)—Reef ⅔ mile from shore doesn't break under 15 feet, sometimes pushes 20. Breaks at most a couple times a year, on a power southwest swell. Hundred-yard-wide peak produces triangle of white water all the way to shore over rock rib extending seaward south of Big Rock. Break can be heard from Windansea, nearly a mile north. Two have tried to ride it, but to knowledge of authors it remains unsurfed as yet. Locals prefer parachute.

(1) Where North Bird Rock might break if the surf were big enough. Other white-water spots are minor peaks of poor quality breaking over the underwater ridge which extends seaward to Hogan's Unprintable. (A) La Jolla Shores Boulevard. (B) Camino de la Costa. (C) Bird Rock Avenue.

NORTH BIRD ROCK (THE FREAKS) — Concentrated peak which breaks top-to-bottom with awesome force ⅓ mile from shore has been described as "the fastest swell in La Jolla, the fastest drop on the coast." Ridable only over 6-8 feet, gets up to 20. Small swells produce unimportant peaks inside. Waves often hard to paddle into, as they may roll all the way inside without breaking. But when they do break, lefts and rights can be equally hair-raising. After initial section, however, lineup is rarely well-shaped. Break is ridable in winter occasionally, good in summer, but best on a "freak" southwest swell. Waves break hardest and have best shape at lower tides. Not blown out easily except by strong winds. Beach and bottom are both rocky, but boards are rarely carried all the way to shore, for waves back off inside. Strong side currents occasionally present during larger swells. Park on Camino de la Costa between Cresta and Cortez Avenues. Surf is in front of cove to south.

(1) South Bird Rock with six-foot surf during a west swell. (A) Bird Rock Avenue. (B) La Jolla Boulevard.

SOUTH BIRD ROCK. [Roy Porello]

Looking from Pacific Beach Point (1) toward South Bird Rock (2), with Zeke's, Haniman's, Rockpile, and Hairmo arrayed from north to south in between.

SOUTH BIRD ROCK—Swells peak up far outside and produce good lefts and rights. The break is gentler than its northern counterpart—the takeoff is steep but the timing less critical. Also the lineup is more fun. However, a rock which sticks up inside when you go right is not gentle, especially in smaller surf. Lefts close out when surf is larger. Begins breaking at about 3 feet, best from 6 feet up, reaches 10. Good mainly on a south swell. Ridable at most tides. Stays glassy longer than other nearby spots after onshore winds start. Area is rocky; expect cut feet, dinged boards. Park at foot of Bird Rock Street. Break is south of the bird rock. Food on La Jolla Boulevard 3 blocks inland.

ZEKE'S—Rights south of the rock which gets in the way when you go right at South Bird. Lose your board and recover the pieces from a cave.

HANIMAN'S (PEGGY'S)—A small shorebreak peak in front of a rocky beach. Fast takeoff. Ride right or left. Best at 3 to 6 feet. Takes most swells with north preferred. Located in front of the private Haniman estate.

ROCKPILE—Thick hard-breaking little peak offers a fast steep takeoff when size is 5-6 feet, with cutback necessary to stay in wave. Three-foot surf is good for hot-dogging. Takes north swell. Beach is what name of place implies. Ocean-front property is privately owned.

HAIRMO—A short fast hollow left, ridable from 2 to 12 feet, best at 6 or more. Rocky beach. Location: just north of Pacific Beach Point.

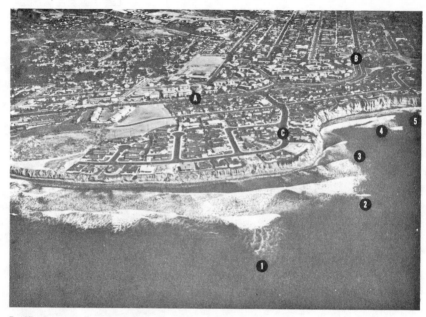

Pacific Beach Point. (1) Outside the Point. (2) The Point. (3) Inside rights. (4) Inside lefts. (5) Old Man's Reef. New Tourmaline Canyon park will be a block to right of picture's edge. (A) La Jolla Boulevard. (B) Turquoise Street. (C) Archer Street.

Lynn Sparks cuts back after the takeoff at ROCKPILE. [Roy Porello]

PACIFIC BEACH POINT (GUNNERY POINT, P. B. POINT, THE POINT)— Swells move in toward north end of point producing surf in four areas as they bend around.

- OUT FRONT (AROUND THE POINT, OUTSIDE THE POINT)—A reef break, a thick wave, ridable above 4 feet, best from 6 to 8, reaches 12. Rights only.

- THE POINT—Thick fat waves—"We used to cheer if they broke." Better at low tide. Mainly rights, occasionally lefts.

- INSIDE—Hot takeoff is followed by well-formed lineup, especially at 4 to 6 feet on medium-to-high tides. Lefts possible in smaller surf, but rights predominate.

- FARTHER INSIDE — Good lefts toward channel.

Area is blown out quickly by south winds, but Inside is somewhat protected from west winds by cliff. At low tide rocks are a menace. Area is best on a north swell, sometimes good on a west, but poor in summer.

Those who enter from Archer Street are trespassing—as retired navy officer who lives here will quickly make clear. Currently only legal entry is by paddling or walking from Law Street, ⅔ mile south. New park planned for Tourmaline Canyon just south of surfing area should provide convenient public access, change rooms, parking, etc.

OLD MAN'S REEF—Takes north swell, ridable from 4 to 8 feet. Wave is neither fast nor slow.

Mickey Madden grabs a rail to pull his board through the wave at the end of a left slide from the peak inside PB POINT.
[Roy Porello]

207

Pacific Beach, with Crystal Pier in foreground. Compare this picture with those of Ventura Power Plant (page 77) and Huntington Cliffs (page 138). All three show typical beach surf. In the other two the waves at the time the picture was taken happened to be ridable, as is clear from the well-defined peaks visible all along the beach. In this shot the straight flat white-water line shows us that the waves are crashing over all at once—no good for surfing today. (A) Mission Boulevard. (B) Garnet Avenue. (C) Mission Bay.

PACIFIC BEACH—More than a mile of good beach surf breaks summer and winter between PB Point and Mission Beach. Ridable size is 2 to 5 feet; smaller surf barely breaks, while larger surf lines up all the way along the beach. Access points from north to south include:

- LORING STREET—Private property adjoins beach.
- LAW STREET (PALISADES PARK)—Law Street is right in the middle of an official swimming area (Beryl to Chalcedony Streets), but surfing is legal outside this two-block stretch.
- CRYSTAL PIER—Area from Diamond to Felspar Streets, north of pier, is an official surfing area with swimming prohibited. Surfers must stay more than 200 feet from pier. Area south of pier (Reed to Hornblende Streets) is reserved for swimming. Peaks near pier may break slightly farther out than along rest of beach.
- SOUTH PACIFIC BEACH—Area from Oliver Avenue to Santa Rita Place, located ½ mile south of pier, is another official surfing area.

Surfing is legal in areas reserved for neither surfing nor swimming if surfers and swimmers stay apart. San Diego City lifeguards on duty in area from 9 AM to 8 PM in summer, 9 AM to 5 PM in winter. Markets, cafes, and restaurants abound.

Close-out day at Crystal Pier, PACIFIC BEACH. [Roy Porello]

Pause on the schnozz. "Skip" Frye entered
camera range on the nose and left it that
way too.—Crystal Pier, PACIFIC BEACH.
[Roy Porello]

MISSION BEACH—Typical beach surf is found winter and summer along the entire two-mile beach, and area may be less crowded than Pacific Beach to the north or Ocean Beach to the south. Surfing is permitted everywhere except in official posted swimming areas; these currently are: Ormond Court to Redondo Court in Old Mission Beach, 400 ft. south of entrance to lifeguard headquarters to Ventura Place in Mission Beach, and Capistrano Place to Deal Court in South Mission Beach.

Official surfing areas (swimming prohibited) are: Nantasket Court to Niantic Court in Old Mission Beach, and Avalon Court to North Jetty of Mission Bay entrance channel.

Area is reached by continuing south from Pacific Beach on Mission Beach Boulevard. San Diego city lifeguards on duty in summer from 9 AM to 8 PM, in winter from 9 AM to 5 PM. Main lifeguard headquarters for San Diego is in Mission Beach.

MISSION JETTY—North jetty of Mission Bay entrance channel produces a left slide from a peak on any swell, with winter swell best. Usual ridable size is 3 to 8 feet; occasionally it reaches 12. Location: South end of Mission Beach. This is an official surfing area (no swimmers).

MISSION BAY—This is undoubtedly the most "mysto" break in Southern California. If a huge west swell is aiming waves straight into the entrance channel of Mission Bay, two- or three-foot rights will form off the west point of Atlantic Cove on the south shore of Tierra Del Fuego, over a mile from the ocean! When everything else is stormy and blown out, these waves will still be glassy and ridable. It must be seen to be believed.

Jerry Jahries powering through a glassy section at the foot of Ormond Court in MISSION BEACH. [Brad Barrett]

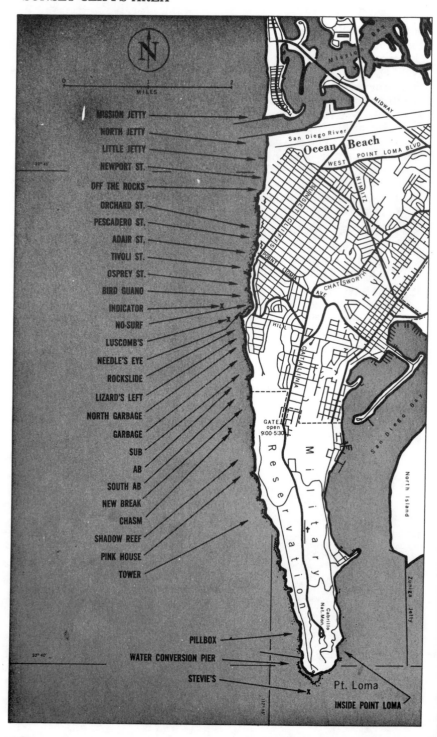

SUNSET CLIFFS AREA

The five miles between Mission Bay and the end of Point Loma offer a larger number of distinct surfing spots than any equal stretch of coast in Southern California. Excepting Ocean Beach, the surf breaks over reefs—often far from shore. Sandstone cliffs rising from the water treat lost boards roughly and the local surfers are especially considerate about retrieving them. Kelp protects the area somewhat from light onshore winds, but the normal afternoon sea breezes sooner or later blow out nearly everything.

The area lies off Highway 101; consult map for access information. Within the area Sunset Cliffs Boulevard is the main drag for surfers. In Ocean Beach it lies a few blocks inland; between Adair Street and the break called "Garbage" it runs right along the ocean. The land on its seaward side there is owned by the City of San Diego and surfing is neither prohibited nor encouraged. Free parking is available in several lots as well as on the street. At many points "taking the drop" down the steep bluffs poses a problem.

Since the surf south of Garbage is in front of land inaccessible to the public (much of it being a super-secret missile testing site), it is rarely ridden even though it is just as good as that farther north. To reach it one must paddle down from the south end of Sunset Cliffs Boulevard.

The only lifeguards, dressing rooms, lavatories, fresh water, markets, cafes, etc., are in Ocean Beach. No camping here or anywhere else in San Diego.

"Taking the drop" down the cliffs usually poses more of a problem than this in the SUNSET CLIFFS area. [Lee Peterson]

Ocean Beach. (1) North Jetty. (2) Little Jetty. (3) Newport Street. (4) Off the Rocks. Every place is hopelessly blown out. Mission Bay entrance channel is calm water to left of North Jetty.

OCEAN BEACH—Nearly a mile of surfable beach front has room for a lot of surfers and there usually are. Surfing areas are:

- NORTH JETTY, which confusingly is the south jetty protecting the entrance to Mission Bay. A right; ridable to ten feet; takes west swell. Takeoff over sandbar is steep, like a reef break. Many stingrays. Surfing allowed at lifeguards' discretion.
- LITTLE JETTY—Peak sometimes forms over sandbar in front of jetty in middle of beach. Takes any swell; ridable to 6 feet. Surfing prohibited when beach is in use by swimmers.
- NEWPORT STREET—Typical beach surf, though the peaks are frequently mushy. Consistent fun waves, reliable on most swells, good to 6-8 feet. The two-block stretch from Santa Monica St. to Niagara St. is an official surfing area, with no swimming allowed; and Newport St. is the social center, abounding with all shapes and forms of gremlins. Muir St. to Santa Monica St. is a swimming area with surfing prohibited. Areas are posted.
- OFF THE ROCKS—Takeoff over reef into left slide on a south swell, with rides up to 300 yards when surf is six-feet-plus. Surfing always allowed.

Location: south of Mission Bay and north of Sunset Cliffs. San Diego City lifeguards on duty in summer from 9 AM to 8 PM, in winter from 9 AM to 5 PM.

Fred Riemann hangs toes, arch, instep and ankle at OCEAN BEACH. [Lee Peterson]

Marilyn Malcolm spins to her left as the board slices through the wave to her right in this perfect reverse kickout during the OCEAN BEACH surfing contest. [Lee Peterson]

"Howdy, y'all." . . . Dave Willingham, OCEAN BEACH. [Roy Porello]

Jim Richards, OSPREY STREET. [Lee Peterson]

(1) Pescadero Street. (2) Adair Street. (3) Tivoli Street. (4) Dumbo's Lefts. (5) Osprey Street, which broke about a minute ago—the foam flecks have not completely disappeared. (A) Sunset Cliffs Boulevard. (B) Adair Street. (C) Osprey Street.

ORCHARD STREET—Slow small lefts and rights. Considered a learning spot.

PESCADERO STREET—Usually much like Orchard Street; good for beginners, but occasionally attains quality at medium-to-high tide with a swell that seems to miss other nearby beaches.

ADAIR STREET—Takes north swell. Rarely ridden.

TIVOLI STREET (GREMMY POINT)—Short lefts from reef near small point crash when over 5 feet, but smaller surf has fair shape.

DUMBO'S LEFT—A reef break outside Tivoli Street when surf is over 5 feet. Messy rip current makes paddling out hard.

OSPREY STREET—Reef break ridable from 2 to 10 feet takes winter swell. Fast takeoffs. Rights long and hot. Lefts bouncier and either fold across or leave surfer inside where he may have tough time pushing through to get back out. Best at low-to-medium tide; high tide makes bad backwash. Rips on either side of peak. Cliffs break lost boards in half without apology. Reef is north of parking lot.

217

(1) Bird-Guano. (2) No-Surf. (3) Indicator. (4) Needle's Eye. (5) Luscomb's. (6) Rockslide. (A) Sunset Cliffs Blvd. (B) Froude Street. (C) Guizot Street. (D) Hill Street. (E) Monaco Street.

NEEDLE'S EYE late in the evening. Vic Takasugi crouches to inspect the mirror finish of his wave. [Lee Peterson]

BIRD-GUANO (correct name unprintable)—Peak builds up fast and comes over hard. Starts breaking at 2 feet, closes out past 6. Lefts preferred. Medium tide best; wave sucks out at low tide. Location: in cove south of Osprey Street parking lot.

NO-SURF—We could just let it go at that. However there are short sloppy lefts and rights ridable from 2 to 5 feet on most swells.

INDICATOR—During smaller swells waves capping over here indicate a set coming in at Bird-Guano, No Surf, and Needle's Eye. But in surf over 7-8 feet one can paddle out ⅓ to ½ mile from shore and ride Indicator's perfect lefts, which may exceed 15 feet. During some swells surf this size breaks more or less all the way across from Osprey Street to Rockslide. Location: Guizot Street.

NEEDLE'S EYE—Spring and fall are the most likely seasons for the west and southwest swells that bring up this fast hollow left. Ridable from 2 to 6 feet; rights acceptable at 2-3. Reefs and cliffs are hard on both boards and people—even by Sunset Cliffs standards. Typical trail to beach (i.e., hair-raising) is 100 yards north of two rock pinnacles near cliff in front of break; these pinnacles, once connected by evidently delicate bridge, account for spot's name. Location: foot of Hill Street.

LUSCOMB'S—Hollow rights and fair lefts. West swell best, north fair. A low tide spot. Hard on boards. Ridable from 2 to 8 feet; larger waves close out. Location: north of Monaco Street.

ROCKSLIDE—Winter break: a left with a challenging and seldom-made section. Takes most swells, reaches 10 feet. Location: foot of Monaco Street.

INDICATOR at very high tide, breaking big and hard but not top-to-bottom. The surfer will be able to steer out of the wave onto the right shoulder. At a lower tide he would not have this opportunity. [Lee Peterson]

Dave Willingham, LUSCOMB'S. [Lee Peterson]

Not Hawaii but ROCKSLIDE. Mike Higgins faces the long lineup. [Lee Peterson]

John Hawley silhouetted in the curl at ROCKSLIDE. [Lee Peterson]

(1) Lizard's Left. (2) North Garbage. (3) Garbage. (4) Sub. (5) Ab. (6) South Ab. Surf is about 5-6 feet and blown out. Garbage, Ab and South Ab are breaking now; North Garbage and Sub broke about a minute ago; and Lizard's Left is not breaking at all. (A) Sunset Cliffs Boulevard. (B) Carmelo Street. (C) Ladera Street.

LIZARD'S LEFT—Hollow but breaks seldom. Location: foot of Carmelo Street.

NORTH GARBAGE (LADERA STREET)—Right; good to 8 feet; any swell, north or west usually better.

GARBAGE (GARBAGE CHUTE)—Breaks from 2 feet up, though wave doesn't attain good quality till 6 feet. It reaches 15 feet and is eminently ridable at that size. Rights on perfectly shaped shoulder are long and always makable; lefts are possible but rarely makable. Best at medium-to-high incoming tide. Takes any swell.

SUB—South or west swell brings up reasonably well-shaped waves ridable from 2 to 10 feet. Rights preferred to lefts. Lost boards seldom carried in to the cliff. Break is named for inshore rock that looks like a submarine.

AB (ABALONE)—Fast well-shaped easy-to-ride lefts from 2 to 10 feet. South or west swell preferred.

The surf immediately south of Ab.

SOUTH AB—Breaks with New Break, but usually 3 to 4 feet larger. Rights preferred to lefts.

NEW BREAK—Hollow rights best on a north swell, all right on a west, definitely poorer on a south. Ridable from 2 to 6-plus feet; larger surf is too fast to make. Best at low-to-medium tide.

CHASM—Straight-up-and-down takeoff into a left slide. Ridable from 5 to 12 feet. West swell. Low-to-medium tide.

AB. [Lee Peterson]

Inaccessible surf near the water conversion plant pier.

By now we're a mile south of the nearest parking place, in territory about which little is known. Three of the breaks in the area are called **SHADOW REEF, PINK HOUSE,** and **TOWER.** In front of a World War II fortification on the military base is a break called **PILLBOX.** South of the water-conversion plant pier visible from Sunset Cliffs Boulevard is an excellent but illegal left. Off the very tip of Point Loma is a place called **STEVIE'S,** a right which breaks on most swells and gets huge, as you might expect of a place so exposed. Also on the east side of the point is **INSIDE POINT LOMA,** a long well-shaped right-slide point surf which is protected from most sea breezes and is best at low-to-medium tide on a strong south swell. The last two spots are like sharksville. In addition to these spots there are probably a couple dozen more which lack generally accepted names because they are so rarely surfed.

Looking north from the tip of Point Loma over uncharted waves. Break in foreground is Stevie's. Lines are building up well beyond the end of the water conversion plant pier, which is half a mile long.

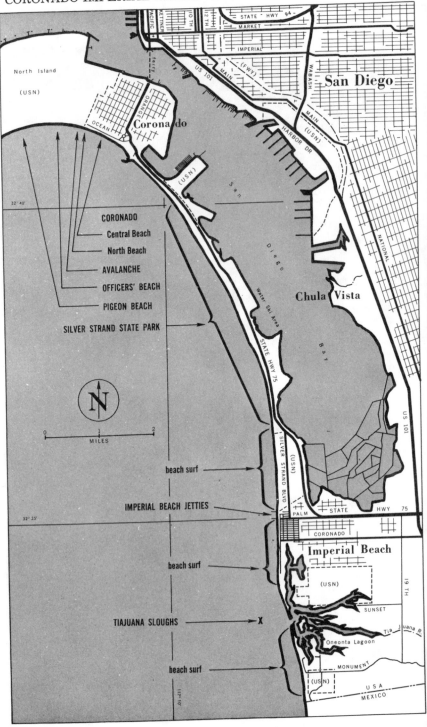

CORONADO-IMPERIAL BEACH AREA

This area is bounded by San Diego Bay on the north and the Mexican border on the south. Most of the coast is sandy beach with fair beach surf all along. Coronado and Imperial Beach are the only towns. The area lies off Highway 101; Coronado can be reached from the north by auto ferry from downtown San Diego, or you may drive directly to Imperial Beach (2 miles) from just north of the border on State Highway 75 and continue northward to Coronado. There are no campgrounds.

Mike Richardson freeboarding at San Diego Bay. The boat is moving about 20 miles per hour, a little slower than for water-skiing. The only limit to time on the nose is gasoline supply.
[Red Richardson]

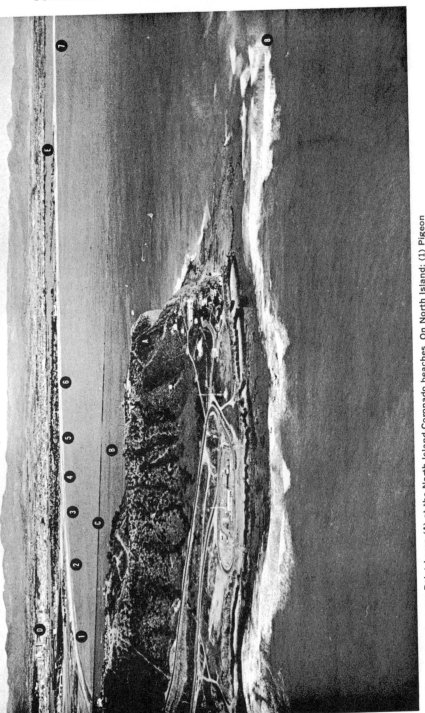

Looking eastward across Point Loma (A) at the North Island-Coronado beaches. On North Island: (1) Pigeon Beach. (2) Officers Beach. (3) The Outlet. (4) Avalanche. In Coronado: (5) North Beach. (6) Central Beach. Farther south: (7) Silver Strand State Park. In the foreground is the break called Stevie's (8). Landmarks: (B) Entrance to San Diego Bay. (C) Zuniga Jetty. (D) Downtown San Diego. (E) San Diego Bay.

NORTH ISLAND (SAN DIEGO NAVAL AIR STATION)—Beach surf all along is best on south swell, with following spots noted:

- PIGEON BEACH—Surf breaks close to shore in front of two sand dunes. Usual sea breeze blows offshore. Located one-half mile west of Officers Beach.
- OFFICERS BEACH—Beach surf. Wind often offshore. Cold water. Open to the public from April to October.
- THE OUTLET—Sandbar break; right wall longer than left.
- AVALANCHE—Another sandbar break, with lefts better than rights. Location: 400 yards west of fence separating naval air station from city of Coronado.

Stingrays at low tide in late summer. Base is reached from Coronado on Fourth Street. Parts of it are open to the public from April to October; hopes are that some portions will soon be open in winter too.

CORONADO—Beach surf favors a south swell, at which time NORTH BEACH (area near fence at north end of beach) is best. Winter swell is likely to be better at CENTRAL BEACH near board rack at Alameda Street. Area blows out fairly easily on south and west winds. Occasional rips. A few stingrays at low tide in summer. Coronado City lifeguard on duty 10 AM to 6 PM in summer south of Alameda Street. Dressing rooms and fire rings on beach. Market at Isabella and Orange Avenues, 3 blocks away. Free parking on streets.

SILVER STRAND STATE PARK—Three or four miles of beach surf. Shore-break good at 2 to 4 feet on a south swell but area takes most swells. Blows out easily. Admission in summer costs 50 cents. Surfing areas are at lifeguards' discretion; lifeguards on duty in summer daily. Entrance to park is on State Highway 75, three miles south of Coronado and 5 miles north of Imperial Beach. Freeboarding is possible in the water-ski area of San Diego Bay just across the street.

Kenny Shurman, PALM AVENUE JETTY, Imperial Beach. Note Point Loma in background.
[Red Richardson]

Imperial Beach Jetties. Surf is 6-8 feet and crashing in unmakable walls. (A) Palm Avenue. (B) First Street.

IMPERIAL BEACH—Jetties at Carnation Avenue and Palm Avenue (in front of lifeguard headquarters) create sandbars over which consistent peaks break farther from shore than along the beaches north and south. Takes both winter and summer swells. Higher tides best. Note rips near jetties. Surf provides fun for the locals when Tijuana Sloughs is not operating. Planned lengthening of these jetties and construction of three more jetties and a pier should further improve waves in the near future. Beach public. Surfing allowed all day. Palm Avenue connects Imperial Beach with Highway 101.

Offshore Santa Ana winds support the curl for Richard Abrams on the south side of the PALM AVENUE JETTY in Imperial Beach. [Red Richardson]

Chip Wilder heads toward the PALM AVENUE JETTY in Imperial Beach. Whether the wave capping over in front of him will crumble down to the bottom or back off depends on sandbar conditions today. [Red Richardson]

Richard Abrams crouches to beat this curl to the safe back-off area near the PALM AVENUE JETTY. Note Point Loma in background. [Red Richardson]

Kenny Shurman banks the board hard in this turn on the north side of the PALM AVENUE JETTY in Imperial Beach. [Red Richardson]

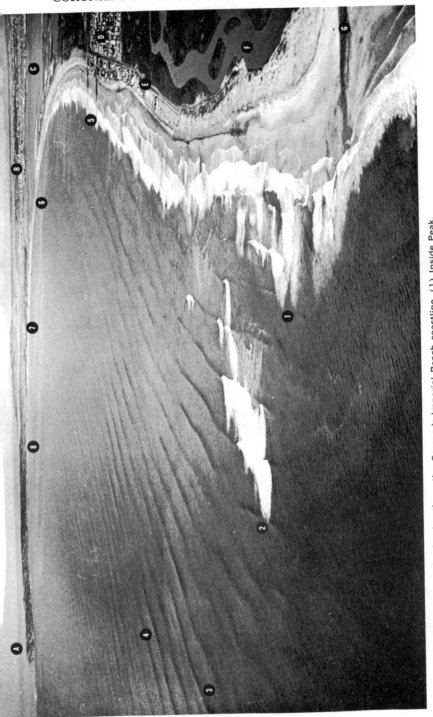

Tijuana Sloughs from the south, showing the entire Coronado-Imperial Beach coastline. (1) Inside Peak. (2) Middles. (3) Approximate location of Outers. (4) Guessed location of Third Reef. Spots farther north: (5) Imperial Beach Jetties. (6) Silver Strand State Park. (7) Coronado. (8) North Island. Landmarks: (A) Point Loma. (B) San Diego. (C) San Diego Bay. (D) Imperial Beach. (E) First Street. (F) Oneonta Lagoon. (G) Tijuana River Mouth.

TIJUANA SLOUGHS—Swells commence to focus on this area far out at sea, break about half a mile from shore, and continue into well-shaped right lineup that allows much turning during a ride of up to 800 yards and terminates in a horrendous shorebreak. In winter this is one of the most consistent big-wave spots on the coast, and wave heights can exceed 20 feet. More specifically, there are the following breaks:

- SHOREBREAK—Unridable in winter but good on medium to large south swells.

- INSIDE PEAK—Starts to break at 6 feet and can be ridden up to 10 feet. Medium tide preferred.

- MIDDLE PEAK—Begins to supersede Inside at 8-10 feet. This break is about ⅓ mile from shore, past the "Back-off Area," where waves whose energy is partially spent can regroup their forces for the shorebreak. Best at lower tides.

- OUTERS (THE NOTCHES)—As surf size grows you paddle farther out. Lining up can be done by positioning the Tijuana Bullring with respect to notches in the mountain range on the horizon, and locals speak of surfing at First, Second and Third Notches. From here the almost legendary THIRD REEF, as yet unridden, may be heard rumbling but not seen (because of waves between you and it) when it caps over at 20-plus feet nearly a mile from land.

Paddle out through fierce shorebreak south of old drainpipe sticking up vertically from water near the beach. After each wave ridden paddle south to channel to avoid being caught inside—these thick waves generate avalanches of white water which can bury the unwary surfer. Thus lefts, frequently possible in surf under 12 feet, are seldom exploited because they leave you in an unenviable position should a set roll through. Area is best on winter swells (except shorebreak). Blown out easily by south or west winds and even by strong offshores; area good only when glassy. Bottom is cobblestones and sand; beach is sand.

Main hazard is high risk of drowning because of distance from shore coupled with size and violence of surf, large amounts of aerated soup which make staying afloat and breathing very difficult, very strong sidecurrents and rips; and cold water. These factors plus frequent fog, absence of landmarks near the water (except that lonesome drainpipe), sound of waves outside growling and hissing, and even occasional visits from killer-whales (inshore from where you sit!) disturb most outsiders' peace of mind and earn spot adjective "spooky." Area is never crowded —perhaps understandably.

Contrary to what name might suggest, Tijuana Sloughs is located in California two miles north of the Mexican border. Imperial Beach lifeguard station, at foot of Palm Avenue, is headquarters for locals. From there drive 1½ miles south on First Street and sandy dirt road (don't get stuck).

Tijuana Sloughs. "Swells commence to focus on this area far out at sea . . ." (1) Inside Peak. (2) Middles. (3) Outers. (4) Third Reef ? ? ? (A) Drainpipe. (B) Parking area.

Tijuana Sloughs — looking south into Baja California. Broken line indicates international border. (1) Inside Peak. (2) Middles. (3) Outers. (A) Tijuana Bullring. (B) Tijuana River. (C) Oneonta Lagoon. (D First Street.

TIJUANA SLOUGHS
Top: Dempsey Holder drops down a small wave at Middles. Center: Dempsey Holder prones out. Bottom: Dick Maxey gives up. Preparing for a half-mile swim he shoves his board to one side, takes a last look at the huge blue wall towering above, and entrusts the next hour of his life to the sea. . . . These three pictures were taken from a boat anchored to one side of the break; it is virtually impossible to take satisfactory pictures from shore. The date is 1956, and the boards were made by Bob Simmons, who spent several years in this area during the early 1950's. [Jim Voit]

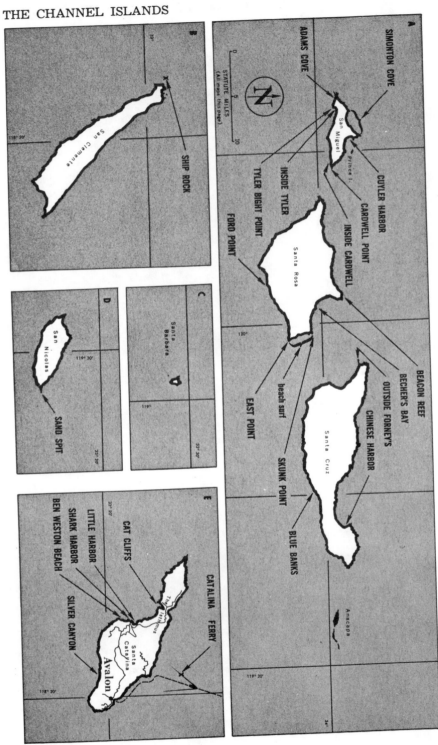

APPENDIX: THE CHANNEL ISLANDS

The islands which block some of the swell from the mainland get plenty of surf themselves. Some of the breaks are almost unbelievable —for example, **CARDWELL POINT.** The west end of San Miguel Island splits the swell, and its two halves bending around the island come together head-on in front of a sand spit at its east end. Here you can sometimes ride one wave north, then turn around and catch another going south; while at other times two waves approaching from opposite directions smash straight into each other in a huge geyser of spray. A body-surfer who rode right into this explosion of soup against soup said he was thrown far into the air. There is a similar spot at the east tip of **SAN NICHOLAS ISLAND.**

These islands offer a variety of big surf. **BEACON REEF** (off Santa Rosa Island) is said to break like Sunset Beach, Oahu; **TYLER BIGHT POINT** (San Miguel Island) like Waimea Bay, Oahu; **OUTSIDE FORNEY'S** (Santa Cruz Island) like a big wave at Dana Point. At **CUYLER HARBOR,** 10-to-20-foot surf which breaks in the channel between San Miguel Island and tiny Prince Island is supposed to resemble big Waikiki. Reliable observers have reported 30-foot surf off **SHIP ROCK** at the north end of San Clemente Island. The prize for sheer spookiness must go to **CORTES BANK,** a shoal about fifteen feet deep located more than 100 miles from the mainland and 50 miles from the nearest land of any sort; imagine the thankless task of surfing its lonely 10-to-30-foot waves in the cold wind and fog. (In the Key Map on page 10, Cortes Bank would be located under the "E" in "North Orange County.")

Nor are the islands lacking in small surf. The east shore of Santa Rosa Island, near **SKUNK POINT,** has excellent beach surf held up by the prevailing westerly winds which here blow straight offshore. **BECHER'S BAY** and **CHINESE HARBOR** on Santa Cruz Island and **SIMONTON COVE** on San Miguel Island are other good beach-plus-reef breaks. **INSIDE CARDWELL** and **INSIDE TYLER** are right-slide point breaks on San Miguel Island, as are **FORD POINT** and **EAST POINT** on Santa Rosa. **ADAMS COVE,** on San Miguel, hosts a small hollow peak; unfortunately it is owned by a colony of seals who usually have priority on the waves.

*The relationship of these islands to the mainland is shown in the Southern California Key Map on page 10.

237

With its peak takeoff near the rock sticking out of the water on the right, SHARK HARBOR on Catalina Island has been likened to Arroyo Sequit. Stalling to let the wave build up is Johnny Fordice.

Precious board-protecting sand — often hard to find in the Channel Islands — is hoarded in the cove on the left, making Catalina's BEN WESTON BEACH a safe place to ride.
[Johnny Fordice]

FORD POINT, Santa Rosa Island, offers a steep takeoff in front of rocks; the ensuing straight-off ride is optional. Clearing the rocks with ease is Preston "Pete" Peterson, probably the first person to surf the Channel Islands. [Leroy Grannis]

Contrary to popular superstition, Catalina too has surf—on its seaward side. Yon don't expect waves at sheltered Avalon Harbor, but **SILVER CANYON, BEN WESTON BEACH, SHARK HARBOR,** and occasionally nearby **LITTLE HARBOR** have good summer surf; while **CATALINA CLIFFS,** near the Isthmus, takes a strong winter swell. Possibly the only islands lacking ridable waves are Anacapa and Santa Barbara, which have sheer cliffs on every side.

Access to these islands, of course, is by boat or plane. Some of them are restricted by the U.S. government for defense reasons. Others are private with permission to land sometimes granted by the owners on request. Only the established harbors on Catalina are available to the general public.

Those who can arrange to go should take wet suits—water temperatures are frequently much lower than on the mainland, at times approaching forty degrees. Also it is understood that the locals (finny variety) are very unfriendly to surfers.

Finally we might mention that the daily steamer to Catalina whips up a large wake, with well-shaped rights off the port side and lefts off starboard. Rides are potentially quite long (26 miles, according to the song), but one is advised not to lose the wave because the "paddle back out" is tiring. Area is blown out by winds from any direction. Good at all tides.

If the skeg of his board misses the ubiquitous kelp, Craig Walker will shoot through one of the bowls at EAST POINT (Santa Rosa Island) and have time to end his ride voluntarily. Otherwise the unmakable final section will do the job for him in a more disorderly fashion. [Leroy Grannis]

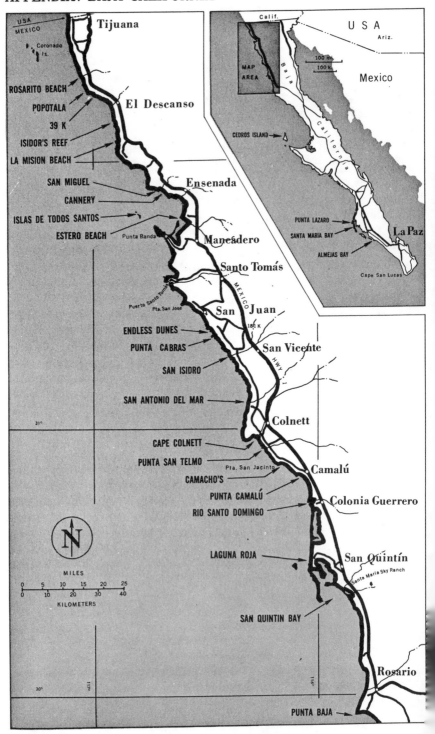

APPENDIX: BAJA CALIFORNIA

Baja California is a goldmine of surf. Far enough south to be out of the swell-shadow cast in winter by Point Conception and unshielded by large islands offshore, this 800-mile peninsula gets waves the year round. Best known to surfers are the 70 miles of coastline between the Mexican border and Ensenada, because paved and well-traveled Mexican Highway 1 is close to the ocean for much of this distance. South of Ensenada, however, surfing becomes more of an adventure; those who would explore owe it to themselves to purchase the *Lower California Guidebook* by Peter Gerhard and Howard Gulick (published by the Arthur H. Clark Company, Box 230, Glendale, California). Its maps and information on road quality are reliable, and its details on places to stay, immigration and customs regulations, history and local color should prove helpful and interesting.

On the main coast route (Mexico 1), distances from the international border are measured by kilometer-posts alongside the highway (1.6 kilometers = 1 mile). Starting at the border you drive quickly (perhaps) through Tijuana and first reach the ocean by taking a detour loop through **ROSARITO BEACH** at 21 K. (However, you could get there by driving west from Tijuana to the bullring and south on a dirt road along the coast). The highway stays near the beach for the next 25 miles, and in this stretch are packed many surfing spots. Among them are **35K** (a rocky point), **38K** (a point), **39K** (a reef with a semi-point farther south), **ELIZIO'S** at 42K (reefs), **ISIDOR'S REEF** at 54K (actually more like a point), and **LA MISION BEACH** at 62 K (beach surf). But should these be breaking poorly or be overcrowded there are dozens of equally good places whose finding requires a minimum of initiative on the part of the surfer.

The highway turns inland at La Mision and does not return to the coast till just north of **SAN MIGUEL** (93K), a point-type surf closed except to members of the United States Surfing Association and to surfers who are clearly not "wild ones." At 96K is the **CANNERY (STACKS),** with a wall surf in front of a breakwater north of the pier, and a peak surf south of the pier. And there are more spots before Ensenada (109K). At 120K a road leads to **ESTERO BEACH,** where surf breaks over the sandbar at the mouth of a large bay—treacherous currents and sharks being among the hazards.

Throughout the area there are stingrays in the water and tarantulas, scorpions and rattlesnakes on land. The water north of 60K is often very cold. The Mexican owners of beach property who admit surfers may make a nominal charge (25¢ to $1.00) for parking and/or camping.

A break called OUTHOUSE, at 38½K. Reason for name is unclear. Structure in foreground is unidentified. It is reported that you can surf both "Outside Outhouse" and "Inside Outhouse." No comment. [Red Richardson]

OUTHOUSE break. Kenny Shurman races the curl in the hope of saving his board from nasty rocks. [Red Richardson]

POPOTALA SHOREBREAK at 32K. Toes belong to Mike Richardson. [Red Richardson]

West of Ensenada 12 miles off the coast lie the **ISLAS DE TODOS SANTOS.** Waves build up in the shallow channel between the two main islands and can be ridden from one end of it to the other.

South of Ensenada and back on land, the paved road continues for 70 miles but is far from the coast. Except for the mostly paved road that leads from Maneadero (130K) to Punta Banda, the routes to the ocean are dirt trails whose viability depends on your vehicle, driving ability and luck. At Santo Tomas (158K) two such roads wind seaward, one to Puerto de Santo Tomas, the other to Punta San Jose and San Juan. At 181K a road leads to good surf below **SAN ISIDRO,** and you can drive north along the coast past rocky **PUNTA CABRAS** to **ENDLESS DUNES,** or south to **SAN ANTONIO DEL MAR** (beach break and pismo clams). There is an enormous amount of good surf in the stretch between **CAPE COLNETT** (233K) and Camalu (260K), including **PUNTA SAN TELMO** (240K), **CAMACHO'S (PUNTA SAN JACINTO), PUNTA CAMALU,** and many reefs that break as much as a mile from shore. The mouth of **RIO SANTO DOMINGO,** near Colonia Guerrero (274K) is a fertile area to search for waves; **LAGUNA ROJA** (298K) offers beach surf and more clams. In summer waves break nearly two miles from shore over the huge shoal at the mouth of **SAN QUINTIN BAY,** while inside breaks are fast with prevailing wind offshore; the area is reached by driving up the hard sand beach from Santa Maria Sky Ranch (313K). Below El Rosario (360K) **PUNTA BAJA** breaks, and the beach surf east of it is held up by offshore "sea" breezes.

Still farther south, surfers who have sailed from California to Mazatlan (located on the Mexican mainland) have surfed at **PUNTA LAZARO, PUNTA MARQUIS,** and **BAHIA SANTA MARIA,** and have reported good waves at **BAHIA ALMEJAS** and elsewhere. Off Cedros Island there is plenty of virgin surf and well-trained cadres of vicious sharks to keep it that way.

And so it goes, all the way to the tip, where "it is reported" that rocky and unsurfable Cape San Lucas has been pounded by waves requiring five seconds to break from top to bottom.

The spots mentioned here may or may not be the best places to surf; they are merely samples of Baja's virtually unlimited surfing potential. The surf of Baja California will be the subject of another volume in the International Surfing Guidebook Series.

SURFING EQUIPMENT AND SERVICES

The following list of California enterprises offering services and equipment connected with surfing is **OBSOLETE**. The names have been included as a memorial to the pioneer businessmen of surfing during the 1960's.

ACME ENTERPRISES (Joe Orcini), 1338-1346 W. 260th St., Harbor City (325-1541). "Acme" boards mfg. Wholesale only: boards, accessories, repairs.

ALLEN SURFBOARDS (John and Al Faas), 4645 E. Anaheim St., Long Beach (433-1353). "Allen" boards mfg. and sale, used boards, kits, accessories, repairs.

AQUATIC CENTER (Al Wood, Ron Merker), 4323 W. Coast Hwy., Newport Beach (673-5440); (Harry Vetter) 308 N. Harbor, Santa Ana (531-6825). Accessories, new and used boards, board rentals.

BING SURFBOARDS (Bing Copeland), 1820 Pacific Coast Hwy., Hermosa Beach (372-1248); 511 E. Whittier Blvd., Whittier (696-1614). "Bing" boards mfg. and sale, used boards, accessories.

BOHEMIAN SURF EQUIPMENT (Jack Rhodes) 1945 Placentia Ave., Costa Mesa (646-0251). "Bohemian" and "Velzy" boards mfg. and sale, accessories. Mainly wholesale.

BORM PLASTIC PRODUCTIONS 325 Motor Way, Santa Barbara (966-6011). Boards mfg. and sale, supplies.

SURFBOARDS BY BRAGG (Bill Bragg), 15209 Daphne, Gardena (324-3711). Surfboards and racing paddleboards mfg. and sale.

CAL-AQUATICS (Herb Hughes), 7423 Lankershim Blvd., North Hollywood (764-7344); (Al Cordle) 21008½ Ventura Blvd., Woodland Hills (346-4799). Retail "Con" boards, used boards, accessories, kits; repairs.

CAMPBELL BOATS (Bill Campbell), 1733 Victory Blvd., Glendale (244-4031). Retail "Velzy" boards, used boards, accessories, kits; repairs.

CAPISTRANO MARINE SUPPLY (Bernard H. Stark), 34664 S. Coast Hwy., Capistrano Beach (496-9221). Retail "Acme," "Holden," "Pomeroy," "Richmark" boards; repairs.

CHALLENGER SURFBOARDS (Bill Bahne, Frank McCleary), 1636 Grand Avenue, Pacific Beach (no phone). "Challenger" boards mfg. and sale, used boards; repairs.

CHOATE SURFBOARDS (Dennis Choate), 750 Iris Avenue, Imperial Beach (424-9473). "Choate" boards mfg. and sale, repairs.

CLARK FOAM PRODUCTS (Gordon Clark), 723 Broadway, Laguna Beach (494-0094). Wholesale only: blanks, foam, stringers.

CLIFFORD SURFBOARDS (Fred Clifford), 4886 La Gama Way, Santa Barbara (967-9725). "Clifford-George" boards mfg. and sale, blanks.

CON SURFBOARDS (Con W. Colburn), 824 Pico Blvd., Santa Monica (396-8224). "Con" boards mfg. and sale. Repairs. Used boards, accessories, kits and blanks.

CRESCENT SURF SHOP (Steward Lambach, Jim Meade), 2524 Colorado St., Eagle Rock (no phone). "Crescent" boards mfg. and sale, used boards, accessories; repairs.

PAT CURREN SURFBOARD CO. (Patrick Curren, Bev Morgan), 413 30th St., Newport Beach (673-5577). "Curren" boards mfg. and sale, accessories.

DUKE DANA SURFBOARDS (Duke Dana), 1811 Sunset Cliffs Blvd., San Diego (no phone). "Duke Dana" boards mfg. and sale, used boards, repairs.

DIVE N SURF (Bill and Bob Meistrell, Harry Pecorelli), 504 N. Broadway, Redondo Beach (379-1473). New boards, accessories.

THE DIVERS DEN (Don Duckett), Breakwater, Marine Center, Santa Barbara (962-4484). Retail "Con" boards, accessories.

THE DIVING LOCKER (Chuck Nicklin), 4825 Cass St., San Diego (488-9088). Accessories; surf photography.

DIWAIN SURFBOARD CO. (Manuel M. Paz), 134 S. Pacific Ave., Redondo Beach (374-9077), 7719 State St., Huntington Park (589-6939). "Diwain" and "Wayne" boards mfg. and sale, used boards, accessories, kits; repairs.

DON'S SURFBOARD SHOP (Don Clark), 838½ Ventura Place, San Diego (488-5730). Rentals; board sales.

DOOLITTLE SURFBOARDS (George Doolittle), 3039 Mauricia Ave., Santa Clara (243-8672). "Doolittle" boards mfg. and sale, used boards, supplies, repairs.

SURFBOARDS BY LARRY FELKER (Larry Felker), 21050 Ventura Blvd., Woodland Hills (340-4555). "Felker" boards mfg. and sale, used boards, accessories, repairs.

FLAHERTY SURFBOARDS (Tom Flaherty, Richard Massey), 7119 Canoga Ave., Canoga Park (348-5370). "Flaherty" boards mfg. and sale, used boards, accessories, repairs.

FOOTHILL SURF SHOP (Doug McKeddic, Ted Duncan), 2934 Frances Ave., La Crescenta (248-2600). Boards mfg. and sale, used boards, repairs, accessories, kits.

FOSS COMPANY (Charles P. Foss), 1767 Placentia Ave., Costa Mesa (646-0244). Wholesale only: foam, blanks, stringers.

GORDIE'S SURBOARD COMPANY (Gordon Duane), 103 13th St., Huntington Beach (536-6050). "Gordie" boards mfg. and sale, used boards, accessories, repairs.

GORDIE'S SURFBOARD COMPANY (Gordon Duane), 103 13th St., Mission Blvd., San Diego (488-7789); (Lee Kiefer, Nick Hanlow) 34186 Coast Hwy., Dana Point (496-1515). "Gordon & Smith" boards mfg. and sale, used boards, accessories; repairs; rentals.

JACK HALEY SURFBOARDS (Jack Haley), 502 Marina Dr., Seal Beach (430-4919). "Jack Haley" boards mfg. and sale, used boards, kits, repairs, accessories.

HANG FIVE SURF SHOP (Earl S. Nickerson), 308 Ocean Blvd., Huntington Beach (536-6905). "Hang Five" boards mfg. and sale, accessories.

HANSEN SURFBOARDS (Don Hansen), 2531 Highway 101, Cardiff-by-the-Sea (753-2100). "Hansen" boards mfg. and sale, used boards, repairs, accessories, blanks.

HARBOUR SURFBOARDS (R. E. Harbour), 329 Main St., Seal Beach (430-5614). "Harbour" boards mfg. and sale, used boards, repairs.

HOBIE SURFBOARDS (Hobie Alter), 34195 Coast Hwy., Dana Point (496-5222); (Chuck Hasley) 1551 Grand Ave., San Diego (274-6014). "Hobie" and "Phil Edwards" boards mfg. and sale, used boards, repairs, accessories, surfing instruction.

HOLDEN SURFBOARDS (William G. Holden) 141 E. 16th St., Costa Mesa (646-4540). "Holden" boards mfg. and sale.

IKE SURFBOARDS (John E. Eichert), 24 W. Cota St., Santa Barbara (No phone). "Ike" boards mfg. and sale, supplies, repairs.

INLAND SURF SHOP (Phil Sauers, Steve Sherer), 7344 E. Florence Blvd., Downey (861-4720). "Phil" boards mfg. and sale, retail "Jack Haley", "Hansen", and "Jacobs" boards, used boards, accessories, repairs.

JACK'S SURF SHOP (Jack Hokanson), 517 S. Brookhurst, Anaheim (533-3209). "Jack's" boards mfg. and sale. Retail "Paul Hunt" boards. Used boards, accessories, repairs, rentals, kits.

JACOBS SURFBOARDS (Hap Jacobs), 422 Pacific Coast Hwy., Hermosa Beach (379-8366). "Jacobs" boards mfg., used boards, accessories, repairs.

PAUL F. LINDEMAN, 8011 Osage Ave., Los Angeles (674-4736). Wholesale and retail: foam and blanks.

MALIBU SURF AND DIVE and **MALIBU PLASTICS CORP.** (James W. Kidd and Willis Todd Carey), 22775 Pacific Coast Hwy., Malibu (456-6037). "Malibu" boards mfg. and sale, repairs, accessories, used boards, rentals, instruction.

MILLIKEN SURFBOARDS (Keith Milliken), 808 Whitley St., Whittier (695-3470). "Milliken" boards mfg., used boards, kits, accessories, repairs.

MIRACLE GLASS CO. (Richard Deese), 620 Cypress Ave., Hermosa Beach (376-4376). Fiberglassing subcontractor, repairs.

SURFBOARDS BY MOSELLE (Ray Moselle Jr.) 11410 Jefferson Blvd., Culver City (391-9139). "Moselle" boards mfg. and sale, used boards, kits, repairs, accessories, fiberglassing.

NEWPORT SURFING CENTER (Larry Tucker) 229 Marine Blvd., Balboa Island (673-9044); 3202 W. Coast Hwy., Newport Beach (no phone). "Tucker" boards mfg. and sale; retail "Dale," "Holden," and "Paul Hunt" boards, used boards, repairs, rentals, accessories, kits.

GREG NOLL SURFBOARDS (Greg Noll), 1402 Pacific Coast Hwy., Hermosa Beach (376-4898). "Greg Noll" boards mfg. and sale, used boards, repairs, accessories, kits and blanks.

OAHU SURF SHOP (D. C. Leedy), 685 Paularino, Costa Mesa (545-6722). "Oahu" boards mfg. and sale, used boards, repairs, accessories.

OLE SURFBOARDS (Bob Olson, Mickey Muñoz), 223 Bay Blvd., Seal Beach (430-2000). "Ole" boards, used boards, rentals, repairs, accessories, kits and blanks, instruction.

OLYMPIC SURFBOARDS (Bill Caster, Bill Wakefield, Phillip Castangola), 3215 Mission Blvd., San Diego (488-8704). "Olympic" boards mfg., rentals, board lockers, repairs, accessories, used boards.

O'NEILL'S SURF SHOP (Jack O'Neill), 1071 41st Ave., Santa Cruz (426-5535); (Bill O'Neill) 2686 Great Hwy., San Francisco (564-4077). "Surf Shop" boards mfg. and sale, used boards, accessories, kits and blanks.

PACIFIC BEACH SURF SHOP (Bernice Capoot), 4040 Mission Blvd., San Diego (488-5445). Retail "Dale," "Holden" and "Velzy" boards, used boards, accessories, repairs, kits and blanks.

PACIFIC COAST SURFBOARDS (Dale Velzy), 6312 W. Coast Hwy., Newport Beach (673-9901). "Dale" boards mfg. and sale, rentals, used boards.

PACIFIC CRAFT PRODUCTS (Harold Abshear), 10106 S. Painter Ave., Santa Fe Springs (693-9012). "Safari" boards mfg. and sale, used boards, kits, accessories, repairs.

PACIFIC FIBERGLASS (Bill May), 2616 Newport Blvd., Newport Beach (675-2540). "Bil" boards mfg. and sale, kits and blanks, accessories, repairs.

PACIFIC PLASTICS COMPANY (William O. Fisher), 182 W. Ramona St., Ventura (653-7003). "Ten Toes," "Tiki," and "Shark" boards mfg. and sale, used boards, accessories, repairs.

PACIFIC SURFBOARDS (Gary Neves, Greg Burrows), 240 9th St., Del Mar (755-4115). Repairs, "Pacific" boards mfg. and sale, used boards.

PLASTIC MART (Ralph Nahigian), 1710 Colorado Ave., Santa Monica (393-4814). Kits mfg. and sale, supplies.

PLASTIFOAM (Jeff White), 2320 Lillie St., Summerland (969-4414). Blanks mfg. and sale, new and used boards, rentals, repairs, kits.

JACK T. POLLARD INC. (Jack Pollard), 511 Cypress Ave., Hermosa Beach (376-3914). Fiberglassing, repairs, kits, supplies.

JOE QUIGG SURFBOARDS (Joe Quigg), 416 31st St., Newport Beach (No phone). "Joe Quigg" boards mfg. and sale, used boards.

ROBERTS SURF SHOP (Robert F. Millner), 214 Culver Blvd., Playa del Rey (398-2026), Roberts boards mfg. and sale, used boards, repair kits, accessories.

SURFBOARDS BY ROSSER, 8038 Freestone, Whittier (696-1616). "Rosser" boards mfg. and sale, used boards, accessories, repairs.

SAN DIEGO DIVERS SUPPLY (William B. Johnston, William F. Hardy Jr.), 4004 Midway Ave., San Diego (224-3439). Accessories, retail "Surfco" and "Velzy" boards.

SANTA BARBARA SURF SHOP (Reynolds Yater), 120 Lillie Ave., Summerland (969-4509). "Yater" boards mfg. and sale, used boards.

SHAN SURFBOARDS (Shannon McCrary), 1001 Olive Ave., Coronado (435-8801). Repairs, "Shan" boards mfg. and sale, used boards .

THE SKAG (Walter Slike, Jim Wells), 54-56 Hermosa Ave., Hermosa Beach (376-2975, 374-9474), "Skag" boards mfg. and sale, used boards, rentals, repairs, storage, accessories.

SURFCO MANUFACTURING CO. (Hoppy Swarts), 10540 Clarkson Rd., Los Angeles (838-3218). "Surfco" boards mfg. and sale, used boards, kits and blanks.

SURFHOUSE GOLETA (Doug Roth), 5832 Gaviota St., Goleta (new phone). Repairs, retail new and used boards.

THE SURF SHOPPE (Colin Lunt), 102 Main St., Huntington Beach (536-8098). Retail new and used boards, repairs, accessories, kits and blanks, rentals.

DAVE SWEET SURFBOARDS (David M. Sweet), 1404-1408 Olympic Blvd., Santa Monica (395-7771). "Dave Sweet" boards mfg. and sale, used boards, kits, accessories.

SURFBOARDS BY TRAVIS (Travis Ashbrook), 16581 Pacific Coast Hwy., Sunset Beach (430-4811). "Travis" boards mfg. and sale, accessories, repairs.

VAL SURF (Bill Richards), 12441 Riverside Dr., North Hollywood (769-4268). Retail "Ole" boards, accessories, used boards, repairs, surfing instruction.

VARDEMAN'S SURFBOARD REPAIR (Sonny Vardeman), 495 Ardmore Ave., Hermosa Beach (376-7464). Repairs, used boards, supplies, fiberglassing.

VENTURA SURF SHOP, 228 E. Meta, Ventura (643-0830). Retail "Ten Toes," "Tiki," "Shark" boards, used boards, kits, accessories, repairs.

HAROLD WALKER CO. (Harold Walker), 1315 N. El Camino Real, San Clemente (492-1391). Wholesale only: blanks, foam, stringers.

WARDY SURFBOARDS (Frederick Wardy), 525 Forest Ave., Laguna Beach (494-0345); 806 E. Colorado Blvd., Pasadena (796-1065). "Wardy" boards mfg. and sale, used boards, repairs, kits.

DEWEY WEBER SURFBOARDS (Dewey Weber), 4116 Lincoln Blvd., Venice (398-0434). "Dewey Weber" boards mfg. and sale, used boards, repairs, accessories.

WEST COAST SURF SCHOOL (Mickey Muñoz), 34320 Coast Hwy., Dana Point (496-5083); also c/o Hobie, Ole, Val Surf. Surfing instruction.

YOUNT SURFBOARDS (Gale and Darrell Yount), 324 Pennsylvania Ave., Santa Cruz (426-1009). Board mfg. and sale, used boards, kits, blanks, repairs.

INDEX TO SURFING SPOTS

Ab 222
Abalone 222
Abalone Cove 129
Abalone Point 152
Adams Cove 237
Aliso Creek 154
Anderson Street 137
Anita Street 153
Ann's 177
Area Zero 89
Armstrongs' Beach 93
Around the Point 207
Arroyo Burro Beach 47
Arroyo Sequit 88
Asilomar 23
Avalanche 125, 229
Avenue "C" 117
Avenue "I" 117
Avila 23

Bahia Almejas 243
Bahia San Quintin 243
Bahia Santa Maria 243
Ballona Creek 108
Ballpark 73
Banzai Shorebreak 197
The Barge 159
Bathtub Rock 187
Bay Street 104
The Beach . . . 86, 129, 155
Beach Barn 183
The Beacon 177
Beacon Inn 183
Beacon Reef 237
Becher's Bay 237
Bee Aye Point 130
Ben Weston Beach 239
Big Dume 91
Big Rock 95, 202
Big Sur River Mouth . . . 23
Biltmore Hotel 50
Bird-Guano 219
Bird Rock . . . 152, 203-205
Bixby Ranch . . . 23, 24-26
Black's Beach 189
Blitzen 52
Bluff Cove 123

Bolsa Chica Beach 137
Bombora 59, 86
Boneyard 159
Boomer Beach 194
Brooks Street 153
Buccaneer Hotel 174
Burn-Down 117
Burn-Out House 117

Cabrillo Beach 130
California Street 73
Camacho's 243
Cambria Pines 23
Camel Point 154
Cameo Shores Cove 151
Camp Pendleton 165-175
Campus Beach 43
The Cannery 241
The Canyon 163
Cape Colnett 243
Capistrano Beach Pier . . . 159
Cardiff Reef 183
Cardiff-by-the-Sea 183
Cardwell Point 237
Carillo Beach 88
Carlsbad 174-175
Carmel 23
Carnation Avenue Jetty . . 230
Carpinteria Beach 53
Carpinteria Reef 52
Casa 194
Cassidy Street 174
Cat Canyon 38
Cat Cliffs 239
Catalina Island 239
Catamarans 174
Cayucos Point 23
Cedros Island 243
Central Beach 229
The Channel 123
Channel Islands 236-239
Chasm 223
Chinese Harbor 237
Church 169
Clobberstones 69
Club Patos al Viento 82
Coal Oil Point 40

INDEX TO SURFING SPOTS

Cockroach 25
Cojo Point 25
Cojo Reef 25
College Point 43
Coral Casino 50
Corona del Mar Jetty . . . 151
Coronado 229
Cortes Bank 237
Cotton's Point 165
County Line 86
County Line Bombora . . . 86
The Cove 123
Crabs 134
The Creek 108
Crescent Bay 152
Croswaithe Street . . . 174
Crumple Car 33
Crystal Cove 152
Crystal Pier 208
Cuyler Harbor 237

D & W's 108
Dahlia Drive 185
Dana Point 157
Dana Strand 155
Del Mar 186
Del Mar Club 104
Del Mar Pier 186
The Depot 160
Devereux's 40
Devil's Slide 191
The Differential 202
Dody's Reef 159
Doheny Beach 159
Donder 52
Drainpipe 90
Drake's Point 33
Dumbo's Left 217
The Dumps 77
The Dunes 40, 174

East Point 237
Edwards Ranch 38
El Capitan Beach 37
El Capitan Point 37
El Morro Trailer Park . . . 152
El Porto Street 110

El Segundo Beach 108
Eleventh Street 186
Elizio's 241
Emma Wood Beach 69
Encina Power Plant 176
Encinitas 178
Endless Dunes 243
Estero Beach 241

Fairground 73
The Falls 155
Faraday's 129
Farther Inside 207
Father John's 67
Fernald's Point 51
Fifteenth Street 186
Fifty-Four Kilometers . . . 241
Figueroa Street 73
First Jetty 173
First Point 59, 94
First Street 110
Five Wells 139
Flat Rock 187
Ford Point 237
Forty-Second Street 142, 143
Forty-Two Kilometers . . . 241
Fourth Street 82
The Freaks 203
The Front 125

Garbage 222
Garbage Chute 222
Gato Canyon 38
Gaviota Beach 35
Giant Rock 89
Glider Field 187
Goleta Point 43
Government Point 24
Grandview Street 177
Greebeland 73
Gremmy Point 217
Guayule 176
The Gully 91
Gully Hole 171
Gumu 163
Gung Ho Shores 169
Gunnery Point 207

INDEX TO SURFING SPOTS

Haggerty's 121
Hairmo 205
Hammond's Reef 50
Haniman's 205
Harrison Reef 86
Hendry's Beach 47
Hermosa Beach 111
Hobson Park 65
Hogan's Unprintable . . 202
Hollister Ranch . . . 23, 27-33
Holly 55
Hollywood Beach 81
Hollywood Bowl 81
Hollywood-by-the-Sea . . . 81
Hope Ranch 45
Horseshoe 197
Hoshi 103
Hubbyland 105
Huntington Beach 139
Huntington Beach Pier . . . 140
Huntington Beach State Park 141
Huntington Cliffs 139

Imperial Beach 230
Indicator 59, 123, 159, 219
The Inlet 83
Inside 43, 125, 170, 207
Inside Cardwell 237
Inside Laguna Point 83
Inside Mushroom 41
Inside Peak 233
Inside Point Loma . . . 224
Inside Solimar 67
Inside Tyler 237
Inspiration Point 129
Isidor's Reef 241
Isla Vista 41
Islas de Todos Santos . . . 243

Jalama Beach 23
Jelly Bowl 53
Jetty Number Five 75
Jetty Number Seven 75
John's Pond 27

K & G Point 130
Kansas City 27
Killer Capo 159
Kolmar Street 201

La Conchita Beach 62
La Conchita Point 62
La Costa Beach 176
La Jolla 189-205
La Jolla Cove 192
La Jolla Shores 191
La Mision Beach 241
Laguna Beach 152-153
Laguna Point 83
Laguna Roja 243
Larry's Place 165
Las Flores Canyon 95
Latigo Canyon 93
Law Street 208
Leadbetter Beach 48
Lefts-and-Rights 27
Leo Carillo Beach 88
Leucadia 177
Lighthouse 103
Linden Street 133
Little Drake's 33
Little Dume 91
Little Harbor 239
Little Jetty 214
Little Point 197
Little Queen's 123
Little Sycamore Canyon . . 86
Lizard's Left 222
Long Beach 133
Longfellow Street 111
Loring Street 208
Los Angeles . 103, 105, 107-108, 130
The Loser 186
Lower California 240-243
Lower Haggerty's 121
Lower Trestle 168
Lunada Bay 125
Luscomb's 219

M & I's 129
Mahaha 151
Malaga Cove 121
Malibu 94-95
Malibu Colony 93
Malibu Pier 94-95
Mandalay Beach 77
Mando's 67
Manhattan Beach 110

INDEX TO SURFING SPOTS

Manhattan Beach Pier . . . 110
Marina del Rey 105
Marine Avenue 110
Marine Street 197
Mary's 67
McGrath Beach 77
Mesa Lane 47
Mexico 240-243
Middle 197
Middle Jetty 108
Middle Peak 233
Mile Zero 171
Miramar Hotel 51
Molino Canyon 35
Monterey 23
Moommy's Mystery 89
Moonlight Beach 178
Morro Bay 23
Mossy Rock 130
Mushroom House 41
Mussel Shoals 62

Naples 39, 133
Naples Beach 39
Naples Reef 39
Needle's Eye 219
New Break 223
Newport Beach 142-149
Newport Pier 146
Newport Street 214
Noah's Ark Trailer Park . . 177
Noche's 27
North Bay 85, 91-105
North Beach 83, 229
North Bird Rock 203
North Boomer 194
North Garbage 222
North Island 229
North Jetty 81, 214
North Point 47, 155
North Reef 123
Northern California 23
No-Surf 219
The Notches 233
Number Seven Jetty 75

Oak Street 73, 153
Ocean Beach 214

Ocean Park 104-105
Oceanside 174
Oceanside Harbor Jetty . . 173
Oceanside Pier 174
Officers Beach 229
Off the Rocks 214
The Oil Piers 63
Old Joe's 95
Old Man's Reef 207
Ooley 224
Orchard Street 217
Osprey Street 217
Out Front 207
Outer Point 59
Outer Reef 91
Outers 233
Outhouse 242
The Outlet 229
Outside 170
Outside Forney's 237
Outside Laguna Point . . . 83
Outside Marine Street . . . 197
Outside Mushroom 41
Outside the Point 207
The Overhead 69
Overhead Shorebreak . . . 69
The Overpass 163
Oxnard Shores 77

P. B. Point 207
Pacific Beach 208
Pacific Beach Point 207
Pacific Grove 23
Pacific Ocean Park Pier . . 105
Paddleboard Cove 123
Palisades 163
Palisades Park 208
Palm Avenue Jetty 230
Palm Street 73
Palos Verdes Cove 123
Paradise Cove 92
Peggy's 205
Pendleton Marine Base . . 165-175
The Pendulum 47
Peppermint Wedge North . . 75
Perko's 24
Pescadero Street 217
The Pier 129

INDEX TO SURFING SPOTS

Pier Avenue 111
Pier Point 129
Pierpont Bay 73-75
Pierpont Jetties 75
Pigeon Beach 229
Pillbox 224
Pink House 224
Pipe 73
Pipes 183
Pismo Beach 23
The Pit 47
Pitas Point 67
Playa del Rey 108
Poche 160
The Point 43, 86, 91, 93, 152, 170, 207
Point Cafe 103
Point Conception 23
Point Dume 91
Point Fermin 130
Point Loma 224
Point Mugu Missile Range . . 83
Point Nicholas 89
Point Sal 23
Point Vicente 125
The Poles 43
Ponto Beach 177
POP 104
POP Pier 105
Popotala 242
Port Hueneme 81-82
Portuguese Bend Club . . . 129
Power Plant . . . 77, 134, 176
Princess Street 191
Pumphouse 197
Pumping Plant 82
Punta Baja 243
Punta Banda 243
Punta Cabras 243
Punta Camalu 243
Punta Lazaro 243
Punta Marquis 243
Punta San Jacinto . . . 243
Punta San Telmo 243
Putty Rock 82

Radar Towers 82
Rainbow Pier 133
Ranch House Point . . . 31

Ratchet 121
Ray Bay 134
Razorback 33
Razor Blades 33
Redondo Beach 117
Redondo Breakwater . . . 117
Refugio Beach 36
Renny's 31
Resort Point 125
Riffraff Reef 160
Rights-and-Lefts 27
Rincon 59
Rincon Bombora 59
Rincon del Mar 59
Rincon Oil Piers 63
Rincon Park Number Five . . 63
Rincon Park Number Four . 65
Rincon Park Number Three . 67
Rio Santo Domingo . . . 243
The Riviera 163
Riviera Club 117
The Rock 91
Rockpile 152, 205
Rockslide 219
Rocky Point 125
Rosarito Beach 241
Rosecrans Street 110
Royal Palms 130

Saint Ann's Street 153
Salt Creek 155
San Antonio del Mar . . . 243
San Augustine Point . . . 27
San Augustine Reef . . . 27
San Buenaventura Beach . . 74
San Clemente Beach State Park 163
San Clemente Island . . . 237
San Clemente Pier . . . 163
San Diego 188-225
San Diego Naval Air Station . 229
San Dieguito Lagoon . . . 185
San Francisco 23
San Isidro 243
San Mateo Point 165
San Miguel 241
San Miguel Island 237
San Nicholas Island . . . 237
San Onofre 170

INDEX TO SURFING SPOTS

San Pedro 130
San Quintin Bay 243
San Simeon Point. 23
Sand Beach 49
Sand Spit 49, 237
Sandyland 52
Santa Ana River Mouth . . 142
Santa Barbara 46-51
Santa Barbara County Line . 59
Santa Catalina Island . . . 237
Santa Clara River Mouth . . 77
Santa Cruz 23
Santa Cruz Island 237
Santa Monica Beach 104
Santa Monica Canyon . . . 103
Santa Monica Pier 104
Santa Rosa Island 237
Sapphire Street 116
Scotchman's Cove 151
Scratchit 121
Scripps Beach and Pier . . 190
Sea Lion 95
Seacliff Reef 65
Seacliff Roadside Park . . . 179
Seafair Lodge 154
Seal Beach Pier 135
Seal Beach Power Plant . . 134
Seaside Reef 184
The Seawall 129
Second Point 59, 95
Second Street 111
Second Trestle 33
Secos 88
Sequit 88
Serena Point 52
The Seven Jetties 75
Seventy-Second Street . . . 133
Sewer 73, 159
The Shack 130
Shadow Reef 224
Shark Cove 51
Shark Harbor 239
Sherman's 177
Ship Rock 237
Shorebreak 233
The Shores 191
Short Street 174
The Sign 160

The Signboard 160
Silver Canyon 239
Silver Strand 81, 229
Simmons Point 197
Simonton Cove 237
Sixteenth Street 111
Ski Jump 123
Skunk Point 237
The Slides 191
Solana Beach 185
Solana Cove 184
Solimar 67
Solimar Reef 67
Solromar 86
Sometime Reef 163
South Ab 223
South Bay 107-117
South Bird Rock 205
South Boomer 194
South Jetty 75, 108
South Laguna Beach 154
South Pacific Beach 208
South Point 155
South Solana Beach 185
Stacks 241
State Beach 103
Steam Plant . . . 77, 134, 176
Steepcliff 123
Stevie's 224
Stone Steps 177
Storm Drain 108
Sub 222
Sun-Gold Point 207
Sunset Beach 137
Sunset Boulevard 103
Sunset Cliffs . . . 213, 217-224
Surf 23
Surf Beach 23
Surfrider Beach 94-95
Surfside 137
Surfside Jetty 136
Swami's 179

T Street 163
Tabletop 184
Tajiguas 35
Tamarack Avenue 175
The Tank 67

INDEX TO SURFING SPOTS

Tar Pits	53	Unnamed beach break	.	24, 65, 67
Terra Mar Cove	176	Unnamed peaks		27
Terra Mar Point	176	Upper Drake's		33
Thalia Street	153	Upper Haggerty's		121
Third Point	95	Upper Trestle		165
Third Reef	233	Utah		31
Third Trestle	33			
Thirteenth Street	136			
Thirty-Eight Kilometers	241	Venice Breakwater		105
Thirty-Eighth Street	143	Ventura		71-75
Thirty-Five Kilometers	241	Ventura County Fairground		73
Thirty-Nine Kilometers	241	Ventura County Line		86
Thirty-Sixth Street	143	Ventura Marina		75
Three Arch Bay	154	Ventura Overhead		69
Tide Hole	69	Ventura Pier		74
Tide Park	184	Ventura Power Plant		77
Tijuana Sloughs	233	Ventura River Mouth		73
Tin Can Beach	137	Victoria Cove		154
Tivoli Street	217			
Todos Santos Islands	243			
Toes Over	108	Washing Machine		81
Topanga Beach	101	Water Tower		137
Torrance Beach	117	The Wedge		148
Torrey Pines Beach	187	West Street		154
Tower	224	Westward Beach		90
Tower Fourteen	139	The Whistle-Buoy		130
Tower Nine	139	White's Point		130
Trafalgar Lane	163	White's Triangle		130
Train Station	160	Will Rogers Beach		103
Trancas Beach	90	Wilson Creek		23
Trestles	165, 168	Windansea		201
Tropics	65			
Twenty-Fifth Street	186	Zeke's		205
Twenty-Second Street	111, 143, 146	Zero		89, 171
Twenty-Sixth Street	111	Zuma Beach		90
Tyler Bight Point	237			